**Advance praise for
Tom Dorsey's Trading Tips—
A Playbook for Stock Market Success
by Thomas J. Dorsey and the DWA Analysts**

"The Dorsey, Wright 'game plan' for investment success is a permanent part of our business. **We don't invest without it!** Tom Dorsey and his associates put years of experience and winning strategy into *Trading Tips*. This book is an ideal gift for our clients."

> NIKKI CHICOTEL
> Senior Vice President, Private Capital Management Group
> Wells Fargo Van Kasper

"**Investing, like football, requires a disciplined game plan.** Dorsey, Wright & Associates' technical analysis offers me and my clients a disciplined approach to investing. This is **a must-read** for both the individual investor and the investment advisor."

> GINO TORETTA
> 1992 Heisman Trophy winner
> Financial Advisor and Quantum Portfolio Manager
> Prudential Securities Incorporated

"Good investment decisions are based on the quality of the information you receive. **Tom Dorsey's approach to technical analysis has been perfected over many years.** Anyone seeking an easily understood book on investing will benefit from Tom's fine work."

> WILLIE LANIER
> Former Kansas City Chief
> Capital Markets Liaison, First Union Securities, Inc.

"Tom Dorsey is the **premier market watcher and master technician. Reading Dorsey's recipes for success is a must.** Here is a guy I read every day—second only to the *Wall Street Journal*."

> FRANK CAPIELLO
> President
> McCullough, Andres, & Cappiello

"For over ten years I have worked with Tom Dorsey to become a **'true craftsman' in point and figure charting.** This playbook will simply speed that process considerably [for other traders]."

> JAMES A. PARRISH, JR.
> President, Private Client Group
> Executive Managing Director, Morgan Keegan Co.

"Point and figure charting provides an X ray of all price movements, and Tom Dorsey in this book **reveals his vast knowledge** of how to run the plays using these charts."

> BOB WOODALL
> Vice President–Investment Officer
> Dain Rauscher

"While Wall Street tries to create a sales force of followers, Dorsey and his crack crew aim to create leaders. Dorsey and crew teach you how to think on your own. **Buying this book is your first step in being a leader, not a follower.**"

> CRAIG M. WIENER
> Senior Vice President
> Wunderlich Securities, Inc.

"As usual, Tom Dorsey has written in a manner that allows both the veteran investor and the novice to **reap the benefits of his knowledge and experience.**"

> JOE STEFANELLI
> Executive Vice President, Derivative Securities
> American Stock Exchange

TOM DORSEY'S TRADINGTips

Also available from
Bloomberg Press

New Thinking in Technical Analysis:
Trading Models from the Masters
Edited by Rick Bensignor

Mastering Microcaps: Strategies, Trends, and Stock Selection
by Daniel P. Coker

Thriving as a Broker in the 21st Century
by Thomas J. Dorsey

Investing in Small-Cap Stocks: Revised Edition
by Christopher Graja and Elizabeth Ungar, Ph.D.

Investing in Hedge Funds: Strategies for the New Marketplace
by Joseph G. Nicholas

Market-Neutral Investing: Long/Short Hedge Fund Strategies
by Joseph G. Nicholas

Small-Cap Dynamics: Insights, Analysis, and Models
by Satya Dev Pradhuman

A complete list of our titles is available at
www.Bloomberg.com/Books

TOM DORSEY'S TRADINGTips

A PLAYBOOK FOR STOCK MARKET SUCCESS

Thomas J. Dorsey and the DWA Analysts

Watson H. Wright, Tammy F. DeRosier, Susan L. Morrison, and James C. Ball

BLOOMBERG PRESS

PRINCETON

First edition published 2001
1 3 5 7 9 10 8 6 4 2

Library of Congress Cataloging-in-Publication Data

Dorsey, Thomas J.
    Tom Dorsey's trading tips: a playbook for stock market success / Thomas J. Dorsey and the DWA analysts, Watson H. Wright ... [et al.].
        p. cm. — (Bloomberg professional library)
    Includes index.
    ISBN 1-57660-077-7 (alk. paper)
    1. Stocks. 2. Investments. 3. Speculation. I. Title: Trading tips. II. Wright, Watson H. III. Title. IV. Series.
    HG4661 .D675 2001
    332.63'22–dc21   00-065108

Edited by Rhona Ferling
Football icon by JoAnne Kanaval

CONTENTS

Acknowledgments xi

Foreword by John Hannah xiii

Introduction 1

Acknowledgments

THE FIRST ACKNOWLEDGMENT from all the authors of this book goes to our families and spouses. It has been an amazing journey for all of us in this company, and you have stood by us all the way. You have understood the nights spent at the office doing research, traveling for seminars, preparing reports, or fixing computers instead of being at home with the family. Your support and encouragement were unwavering through the tough times, and we're ever so grateful that you were there for the good times, too. You have allowed each of us to foster our passion for point and figure technical analysis, and for that we owe you a debt of gratitude. All of you are the absolute greatest.

These acknowledgments would not be complete without recognizing some very special people who were integral in making the book come to fruition. Mike Moody and Harold Parker, Dorsey, Wright Money Managers, we thank you for your help with some of the tips, along with your advice and consultation on point and figure analysis over the years. J.P., without your terrific editing and critiques, this book would not read so eloquently. We are very grateful for the many hours you spent proofreading and making suggestions.

Erica Wooten, we could not have gotten this manuscript together without you. Erica began working with us as an administrative assistant three years ago. After a year, she went back to school to finish her degree and has continued to work part-time with us. We sincerely thank you for doing all of the chart work for this book. We would also like to acknowledge Jim Simcoke, who took time out of his busy schedule to read this manuscript and give his insight, as well as John Hannah, who wrote the foreword. Clients like you, who share the same desire as we do to study the markets and help our clients, are the reason we stay fired up.

FOREWORD

BY JOHN HANNAH

ON A SUN-FILLED SUMMER DAY in New England, I was on my way to see a client. It is my practice to meet with clients regularly to review their portfolios and share my views on the market. I was reviewing the Dorsey, Wright daily market indicators and the point and figure charts for each holding in my mind when I received a call on my cell phone. It was Watson Wright. He asked me if I would write the foreword for a new book his firm was authoring. At first, I felt a little intimidated.

However, those feelings immediately subsided as I remembered what stock analysis used to be like. Before I became familiar with point and figure charting, I felt like a parrot. I simply memorized what the research reports said and very little more. Essentially, I had no control over my portfolios and ultimately my business. I was totally dependent on our analysts. Our analysts are very good at identifying the best companies within their assigned group. My problem was knowing when to purchase their recommendations.

Now fast-forward to that New England summer day. Here I was filled with assurance, knowing that I was creating value for my client and happy to be sharing my views. What caused this transformation? To help you understand, I need to give you a little background.

I became interested in the market in the '70s while playing in the National Football League. When the World Football League began to hire players away from the NFL, salaries became high enough for me to start thinking about investing (this should have been my first clue that supply and demand control prices). Mr. Tom Phillips, a friend of several New England Patriot players and president of Raytheon, served as a board member of a prominent Boston investment management company. He arranged a meeting for the players to learn the basics of investments from several of the money management company's leading portfolio managers. I was hooked! Shortly after that meeting, I began to invest in mutual funds and generally to follow the market.

Toward the end of my football career, I decided I wanted to make Boston my permanent home. I needed to find a way to earn a living after football, so I turned my avocation into my vocation. In 1983, I joined L. F. Rothschild, Unterberg, and Tobin. My goal was to become a top-notch investment adviser. I began a company named The Hannah Group, and with the help of several qualified and loyal associates and friends, we became an investment consultant to many of the commonwealth's public retirement systems. In 1996 I sold my firm, and due to conditions beyond my control, I turned to my first love—managing stock portfolios. After all, for the previous ten years I had observed and studied the quantitative and qualitative analysis used by many of the world's top investment advisory firms. I thought that all I had to do to succeed was use the analytical tools that had proven successful for the best of these firms. However, something was missing.

I became a disciple of Peter Lynch when a mutual friend, Dr. Armand Nicoli, arranged a luncheon meeting. I remember the meeting as if it were yesterday. I came to the restaurant armed with pen and paper, prepared to spend the rest of the day being tutored by the person I admired most in the business. The first thing he did was to tell me to put away my writing materials, and he then proceeded to teach me the same lessons which have now been published. I made his philosophy my own, but after a less-than-stellar quarter, I decided to review my investment process and compare my procedures with those outlined by my investment hero. I thought I had followed his guidelines explicitly. However, as I was again flipping through articles, books, and everything else I had filed on Peter Lynch's investment philosophy, I noticed a picture of Mr. Lynch with a chart book in hand. Was technical analysis the missing ingredient?

A COLLEAGUE HAD SUGGESTED earlier that I should read *Point and Figure Charting* by Tom Dorsey, so I went to the bookstore. As I read his book, I realized I had forgotten the basics of economics—supply and demand control prices. When I played football, many teammates thought I was crazy. I spent hours before and after practice perfecting my stance. A football stance is the beginning point of everything an offensive lineman does. From your stance you either drive block, pass protect, or pull. If you do not put your body in the correct position at the beginning of the play, nothing else will work. I had forgotten this elementary point when investing. I had tried to run the play without getting in a good stance.

I needed coaching! I called Dorsey, Wright first thing Monday morning. I asked when they were going to conduct their next class on point and figure charting. The next class was full, but after several minutes of begging and pleading, they allowed me in. This humbling of myself was well worth it. The time I spent in Richmond was the beginning point of getting my portfolios into position to beat the market. The basic principle they taught, that the weighting by asset class (cash vs. stocks) and by sector have more impact on portfolio performance than the individual stock selection, was borne out by my experience as a consultant.

What they taught me was to identify the risks in the market and within the sectors of the market. I also learned how to identify when to buy stocks at attractive entry points. Nevertheless, I continue to learn and hone my skills. Since that class, not a day has gone by that I do not read Dorsey, Wright's "The Daily Equity and Market Analysis Report." I read it not so much to glean profits from their trading ideas but to learn new lessons on how better to identify the forces of supply and demand on the market.

Today, just as I did when playing football, I return to the basics before every trading day. I religiously follow the five-step investment process outlined by Dorsey, Wright, plus one of my own:

1 I review the risk in the market by determining whether or not I should be playing offense or defense. As they have taught, the market is like the tides of the ocean. When the tide comes in, all stocks tend to rise, but when the tide goes out, they all tend to go down.

2 I determine which economic sectors are the most favorable.

3 I review my portfolios to determine which holdings are controlled by demand and which holdings are controlled by supply.

4 I study our daily analysts' comments to maintain my list of fundamentally sound companies.

5 I then review those recommended stocks to find those that are strong on a technical basis (demand is in control).

6 Lastly, I decide if any portfolio holding should be replaced with a recommended stock due to a better risk/reward relationship.

SINCE ADOPTING THIS PROCESS, my portfolios have more consistently outperformed the market, I have gained new confidence in my selection process, and I have been better able to communicate my approach to clients and prospects. All this combined allows my clients and prospects to have greater trust and confidence in my abilities to help them reach their investment goals.

In football, your offensive package may feature the run or it may feature the pass. In either case, the first thing you must develop before you can become a good offensive lineman is a stance. It is the basis from which all else starts. In the same way, whether you are a momentum, growth, or value investor, supply and demand control price movements. If you don't get your portfolio in the right stance, where demand is in control, you're less likely to beat the market. I would suggest that you take the lessons taught in this book to heart and use them as a starting point to improve your chances of investment success. Remember, however, that this is just the beginning and that champions always continue to improve their abilities.

—JOHN HANNAH
First Union Securities
Andover, Massachusetts

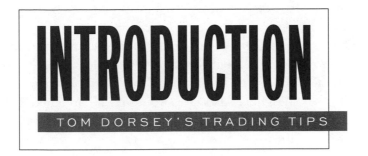

INTRODUCTION

From Dream to Reality:

The Evolution of Dorsey, Wright & Associates

I'LL NEVER FORGET that dark, cold day: January 2, 1987.

Reality had struck. This was the first day Dorsey, Wright &

Associates (DWA) was in existence. I had just left as Senior

Vice-President/Director of Option Strategy at Wheat, First

Securities. I had a pregnant wife and two young sons. My

net worth was in the $20,000 area, and I was scared.

Watson Wright, the partner who had been my right-hand man in my Options Strategy Department, was meeting me in the coffee shop of the building that housed our 250-square-foot office space. That was the headquarters of Dorsey, Wright & Associates. We had a secretarial desk, a Tandy 3000 leased computer, two chairs, and a couch.

That was the ball game—not many tangible resources, but tons of hope. We'd been able to secure a $90,000 loan from Dominick & Dominick Brokerage firm in New York. Without them, I'm not sure Dorsey, Wright & Associates would have happened. It didn't take us long to pay Dominick & Dominick back with interest. We were on our way.

The decision to make the cut from Wheat, First Securities was a difficult one. It's hard to give up a high management position at a solid firm for something that might or might not materialize. I knew for a very long time that my own personal cutoff date to start my own business was age forty. The closer I got to that age, the more I felt the urge to make the break. I knew that at the age of forty I could try and fail and still have plenty of time to regroup and head in another direction. That decision becomes much more difficult at fifty. My children would be moving out of high school and into college, and I knew I would need a much more secure life at that time. I also needed my wife to be behind me 100 percent. She was the one who was pregnant with our soon-to-be baby girl. That was no problem, as Cindy knew it would eventually turn out to be the best decision for the family. She could always see things in me that I could not.

Once I decided to make the break, take the loan from Dominick, and start my new company, I brought Watson into the equation. I knew I would need a partner to accomplish my goals, and Watson was my choice. We had worked well together for many years in the Options Department, and this was simply the next logical extension of that relationship.

I remember broaching the question with Watson. It was cold-sweat time. I dropped it on him like a bomb. I was heading for the gate and wanted him to be my partner. He said he would think it through.

It was a tough decision, as he would surely take over the department and move up the corporate ranks. Wheat, First Securities was a great firm to work for, and becoming head of options strategy was tempting. It took Watson about a week to think it through and then to go. We turned in our resignations. I needed some time to find a suitable replacement for myself in the department and was able to do so with an institutional salesman at Wheat, First. Consequently, we left on great terms with Wheat, First Securities, and they became our first client.

What we intended to do had been tried only once before by another group, and they had failed. We wanted to become Wall Street's first outsourced Options Strategy Department. We planned to reproduce at Dorsey, Wright the laboratory we had created at Wheat and provide solid options strategy to firms that otherwise would not have that capability. You see, I was a member of the regional brokerage firms' Options Round Table. I knew all the heads of all the regional brokerage firms' options departments. They were the most overworked group of professionals on Wall Street. Most of them wore many hats in their departments; I was always in awe of how they got all of their jobs done.

The one deficiency I saw in many of these departments was strategy ideas. This is exactly where we excelled. At Wheat, I was responsible only for providing ideas and strategies on listed equity options. This fit perfectly with most regional firms.

Well, we started taking on one account at a time. We had a good day if someone returned our call. It didn't take much. After Wheat, First, we convinced Rauscher Pierce to come aboard, then Alex Brown, and J. C. Bradford, and the ball started rolling. It started to look like we just might make it. "Making it" to us was simply earning a basic salary and being our own bosses. If we could do that, we had succeeded. Well, it eventually turned into much more than that.

Our big lift came from securing a trading client with the largest European hedge fund. Not only did this give us a tremendous confidence boost, it also resulted in so much business we were able to pay off our outstanding loan.

It wasn't all roses, though. Susan Morrison had just joined the firm in late September 1987, coming over from Signet Bank's Municipal Bond Department. She was very excited to get back into the stock market and leave those boring bonds behind. If going to school full time and working at Dorsey, Wright weren't enough, along came October 1987, and it was baptism by fire for her.

We'd only been in business for ten months when the crash of October 1987, "Black Monday," occurred. This was a defining moment in our business. What happened that day changed the options business forever.

The market had been so good since 1982 that most options traders became totally and unequivocally complacent. In fact, the market had been so good that in their eyes, it only went up. Many options traders had begun to sell uncovered puts. Why not? Selling uncovered puts is a strategy that is perfectly designed for rising markets. Selling a put option is like underwriting insurance. In other words, if all cars in America never had any accidents, the best business to be in would be the insurance business. You would never have to pay off on any claims.

This is what happened with option investors. They all decided to enter the underwriting business of insuring stocks. If they never went down, the insurance (uncovered put) would expire worthless, and the investor would always keep the premium.

That was all well and good until the fateful day of October 19, 1987: Every car in America had an accident. Those who chose to underwrite those cars had to pay off on the insurance claims. It was a disaster. What was a nice, secure little business selling uncovered put options came home to roost. Massive losses were generated on Wall Street. Individual investors all of a sudden didn't understand the risks associated with selling uncovered puts, and lawsuits against their brokers for unsuitable recommendations were coming out of the woodwork. In one day the options product went from being the darling of Wall Street to a potential hazard to be avoided at all costs.

On that day, our business changed dramatically. I knew that the options business would never be the same again. We took the term *options* off of our name and disavowed all knowledge of the options product. Since we were always self-contained, doing our own research using the point and figure method, we began calling ourselves a technical analysis firm. That was exactly the right move, and our business expanded from there, with our main focus becoming the point and figure methodology. Our goal was to become known as the point and figure experts. This opened a whole new, wide world for us to develop.

For this to happen, we had to continue to add quality associates as the research needs and client base expanded. As if one fixed-income dropout weren't enough, along came Jay Ball in October 1990. He had recently moved back to his hometown of Richmond, relocating from New York City. In New York, he had worked on PaineWebber's Taxable Fixed Income desk. Like Susan, Jay saw great opportunities in Dorsey, Wright and preferred equity market analysis.

During this same period, Tammy DeRosier was our first summer intern. She started in the summer of 1988 and worked summers and holidays, sharpening her analytical skills. Upon graduation in 1992, she joined the company on a full-time basis. Watson and I, along with Susan, Jay, and Tammy, were the backbone of Dorsey, Wright & Associates for the better part of the nineties.

Over the years, our business grew into a truly international firm. Up until 1997 it was this core group of five people that put in fourteen-hour days, worked weekends, and did whatever else needed to be done—from taking out the trash to answering the phone, and above all, providing consistent, quality research.

You see, the five of us believed in Dorsey, Wright's purpose—that of educating, advising, and motivating brokers and money managers around the world in the point and figure methodology. This commitment to excellence has helped us to make a difference in countless brokers' and investors' lives. The company has now grown to ten employees, several college interns, and two money managers who run Dorsey, Wright Money Management. Keeping up with the Internet revolution, Dorsey, Wright & Associates maintains the largest point and figure database available to professional and individual investors at www.dorseywright.com. This database provides the tools to help use many of the trading tips discussed in this book, as well as timely updates from the Dorsey, Wright analysts.

Educating our clients has always been a key focus at Dorsey, Wright. During the last fourteen years we have taught numerous courses on the point and figure methodology worldwide. We have a two-day Stockbroker Institute where we teach our clients to become craftsmen in this form of technical analysis.

We view these instructional courses as teaching an operating system. Computers and automobiles have operating systems to function, and similarly, investors and brokers must have an operating system to succeed on Wall Street. We provide the operating system for success in investing and then back up our clients as if we were their own personal technical analysis department. We field hundreds of calls and e-mails each day. Providing solid, up-to-the-minute support to all of our clients is what makes us different.

As the company has grown, we have embraced new types of technology, and most importantly, we've learned from our experiences. Since Dorsey, Wright's inception, the five of us have collaborated to write approximately 3,500 daily research reports that encompass twenty pages each. That's 70,000 pages of handwritten research over the years. Every day each analyst talks to or e-mails over fifty clients. That's approximately 875,000 conversations about individual stocks, option strategies, the bias of the market, interest rates, etc., with brokers, traders, and money managers all over the world throughout the years.

Each one of the five analysts writing this book has charted, by hand, over 1 million point and figure charts. Together, that's about 5 million point and figure charts updated by hand. I wouldn't even gander to guess how many Xs and Os that would be handwritten into charts! This doesn't even take into account the other chart patterns we have looked at on the computer screen. We've calculated that each one of us has averaged 62,400 handwritten or typed technical comments on individual stocks or about 312,000 comments among the five of us. And we're still going strong!

In a world in which everyone is trying to be an also-ran, our experience in the market is what makes Dorsey, Wright & Associates stand out above the crowd. We have aggregated some of the most important and interesting tips in this book. It's a culmination of lessons from our many research reports, updated chart patterns, comments, and conversations. We bring these experiences to you in the form of this *Trading Tips* book.

Because we are point and figure experts, many, but certainly not all, of the tips that follow relate to this form of technical analysis. Therefore, if you are not familiar with this methodology, we suggest you take a few minutes to read the point and figure tutorial located in Chapter 1, or consider reading my first book, *Point and Figure Charting: The Essential Applications for Forecasting and Tracking Market Prices.*

In the following pages you will come to understand how fourteen years of immersing ourselves in the markets, and specifically the point and figure methodology, has made us true craftsmen in technical analysis. We hope that this book will bring you closer to becoming an expert, too.

CHAPTER

BUILDING A FOUNDATION:
POINT
AND
FIGURE
BASICS

ONE OF DORSEY, Wright & Associates's missions is to provide investors with a solid game plan for investing. Before being able to understand the entire playbook, you must first learn the rules of the game. In this first chapter, we lay out the basic rules of our research methodology, point and figure charting. Just as it is important for football players to attend summer camp to get ready for the upcoming season, so too is it advisable for you to understand the basics of point and figure charting before starting your season of investing. Veterans, alongside rookies, attend summer camp each year, honing and polishing their skills. This chapter will serve as an essential review for veterans, while also teaching the rookies.

PLAY # 1

Why You Should Combine Technical with Fundamental Analysis

*Playing the piano with two hands is better
than playing it with only one.*

OFTEN, ONE OF THE FIRST questions an investor asks is "What stock should I buy?" This question can involve a great deal of time and analysis. In many cases, the average investor will want to find out what the company does; review its financial statements; see if it pays a dividend, as well as how long that dividend has been paid and whether or not it will continue to be paid; discover whether the company's earnings are rising or falling; analyze its products; and so on. In other words, the investor does a great deal of fundamental research to find out if that stock is the one to purchase.

This analysis answers the question of *what to buy*. However, it says nothing of *when to buy*. The best stocks have periods when they perform worse than the market, just as the weakest stocks have times when they perform better than the market. If no one is going to buy the so-called best stocks, then they are not going to rise. On the other hand, if a large number of investors buy a fundamentally weak stock, then it is headed higher.

At DWA we use point and figure charts to determine when to buy stocks. By charting stocks with this method, we see the movement that determines whether supply or demand is in control of the stock. If it is supply, then the probability is high for that stock to decline. The odds favor a rise in the price if demand is winning the battle. You will also want to keep in mind that there are no disinterested investors. Back in the 1920s, there was no Securities and Exchange Commission to regulate companies and when and what they reported. Rumors were rampant, and it was not surprising to see wealthy and knowledgeable investors pool their money to trade. These pools gave them a huge advantage over the individual investors.

Today the Internet creates stock movement. There are chat rooms everywhere and practically anyone can offer ideas. Remember that the person who is wildly promoting or recommending a particular stock more than likely already owns it. You will also want to keep in mind that the investor who is badmouthing a stock has probably just sold that stock or has sold it short, hoping to buy it back at a lower price.

In this environment, you need something that will help you sort through the morass of opinions out there to determine whether demand or supply is in control. We recommend using technical analysis, preferably the point and figure methodology. Let the fundamental analyst help determine what you buy. But let the technical analyst determine when you buy that particular stock. When the market is topping, typically the news stories are all good, and that is not *when* you want to buy. ❏

PLAY # 2

Why We Use Point and Figure Charts

Go with what you know and what you believe in.

MANY PEOPLE HAVE ASKED why we use point and figure charts instead of bar charts or candlestick charts or some other technical method. We have no arguments with those who choose these other methodologies. For example, an experienced practitioner of bar charts can probably do quite well with them. But we feel that constructing bar charts is far more difficult and time-consuming. True, they show volume, and P&F charts do not. However, with so much computer trading, not to mention the new online trading, analysis of volume can be a somewhat deceptive and precarious process. In any event, if the volume is sufficient to cause a significant movement in price, this movement will be clearly reflected on the P&F chart.

Besides being difficult to read, daily bar charts can also easily cause confusion. You can frequently get bogged down in trivia and lose sight of the overall picture. While keeping weekly or monthly charts on the same stocks can remedy that problem, it is more difficult to do. Not only that, but if you ask five different bar chartists for their opinion on a single stock, the odds are you will get five different answers. It is kind of like taking an inkblot test. Everyone can start with the same information, but come up with entirely different results. In our opinion, P&F charts will give you both an immediate and long-term view, all in the same chart. And getting one opinion from five people is the norm, not the exception. Listed below are the reasons we think point and figure charts are superior.

1 Formations are easier to recognize and interpret. The patterns tend to repeat themselves.

2 Trends are readily identified, and trend lines can be drawn with amazing ease.

3 Valid targets can be established using the vertical and horizontal counts.

4 With one tool, the technician can see both the near-term and long-term position of a stock.

5 It is the easiest kind of chart to keep, and therefore allows you to follow more stocks. Although it is difficult to keep bar charts of fifty or one hundred stocks by hand each day, keeping that many point and figure charts up to date is relatively easy. Charting by hand every day also gives you a good feel for the stock, a feel you would not otherwise get.

6 It enables the investor to do what he should do—stay on a winner while it is winning and get off a loser quickly.

7 The pricing interval we use may be made to fit whatever you want to chart—stocks, bonds, commodities, speculation, or investment, as well as volatility. ❏

Point and Figure Chart Basics

Before you can put the roof on the house, it must have a solid
foundation to support it. The same is true for investing.

THE POINT AND FIGURE METHODOLOGY has been around
for over one hundred years now. One of the first proponents of
the methodology was Charles Dow, first editor of the *Wall Street
Journal*. We all know that Charles Dow was a fundamentalist at
heart, yet he appreciated understanding the supply and demand
relationship in any stock. The point and figure methodology is just
a logical, organized way of recording this relationship.

We all understand this simple economic theory; it's Economics
101: We know why, in the winter, tomatoes that don't taste very
good and that don't have a very long shelf life are, nevertheless,
expensive. The same forces that move prices in the supermarket
affect stock prices. When it's all said and done, if there are more
buyers than sellers willing to sell, the price will move higher. If
there are more sellers than buyers willing to buy, the price will
move lower. If buying and selling are equal, the price will remain
the same.

Some of the first point and figure charts were constructed by
taking a piece of graph paper and recording the price of the stock
in each box. For instance, if a stock was trading at $50, then the
figure 50 would be written in one square. If the stock then traded
up to $51 the next day, a 51 would be written. If the stock began
to fall in price, the chartist would move over a column and begin
recording the figures 50, 49, 48, and so forth (**EARLY POINT AND FIG-
URE CHART**). Over the years, the point and figure methodology has
developed, and now the prices are put on the vertical axis and the
numbers or figures have been replaced with Xs and Os (**MODERN
POINT AND FIGURE CHART**). Simply stated, Xs stand for demand and
are always moving up the chart, while Os stand for supply and are
always moving down the chart. Here are the basic tenets of a point
and figure chart; see **EARLY POINT AND FIGURE CHART** and **MODERN POINT**

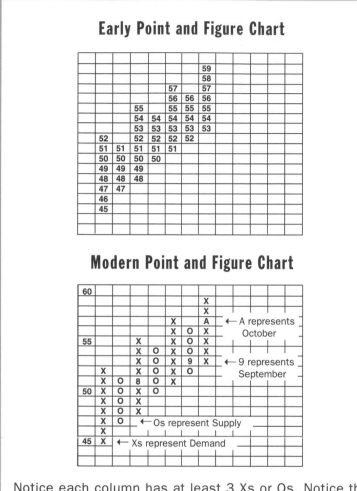

Early Point and Figure Chart

Modern Point and Figure Chart

Notice each column has at least 3 Xs or Os. Notice the columns alternate between Xs and Os.

AND FIGURE CHART, above:

◆ The daily high and low price each day is used to record the chart movement.

◆ Columns of Xs and Os alternate.

◆ Xs and Os are never mixed in the same column.

◆ There must be at least three Xs or Os per column.

◆ The numbers in the chart record time and identify the months of the year. For instance, 1 represents January, 2 represents February, 3 represents March, and so forth through September. A, B, and C are used to represent October, November, and December respectively. ❏

Point and Figure Tips

Don't be afraid to get your hands dirty.

WE TEACH SEMINARS ABOUT point and figure charting all over the country. At these seminars we teach the basics of point and figure charting to both stockbrokers and investors. It is during these seminars that we advocate P&F charting by hand because you learn more about the method, and you see exactly what takes place in the stocks you are charting.

We liken it to the pottery maker. You have probably seen pictures of one of these artisans, sitting at a wheel and using her hands to make a beautiful piece of pottery. If she moves her hands too much the pot is ruined, and she must begin anew. She does not just sit down and on the first time at the wheel come up with a masterpiece. It takes work, practice, and skill to produce these works of art.

Compare that to machine-made pots. These are mass-produced on an assembly line. Yes, they are all uniform and not as expensive. But then again, the handmade pots are one of a kind and combine the skill, the art, and the passion of the craftsman.

Certainly if you are new to the point and figure method, then charting by hand will help you learn the basics much faster. Take a handful of stocks and begin charting these by hand each day at the close of the stock market. Do not select one hundred or two hundred stocks to begin your experimentation. That's too many. You may graduate to that many down the road, but do not start there. It's similar to being out of shape and deciding to work out and tone up. You do not go out the first day and run ten miles. You start slowly and gradually work your way up to the level you want. If you start too fast, you will end up miserable and in pain,

Bullish Chart Patterns

Double Top

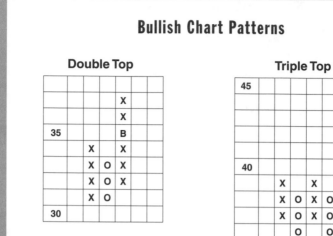

Triple Top

An X (up) column exceeds the previous X (up) column. The simplest of all buy signals.

An X column exceeds two previous columns, or levels of resistance.

Bullish Catapult

Combination of a triple top buy signal followed by a double top buy signal.

Shakeout

50							
					X		
					X		
					X		
		X		X	X		
45		X	O	X	O	X	
		X	O	X	O	B	
		X	O	X	O	X	
		X	O		O	X	
		X			O		
40							

Bullish Triangle

40					X			
					X			
		X			X			
		X	O		B			
		X	O	X	X			
35		X	O	X	O	X		
		X	O	X	O	X		
		X	O	X	O			
		X	O	X				
		X	O					
30		X						

Stock makes two tops, then breaks a double bottom. This rids stock of weak holders. Can buy on three box reversal up. Shakeout is completed when triple top is broken.

Series of lower tops and higher bottoms. Chart breaks out one way or the other. Take action on breakout, but not until then. Five columns are required to make the pattern.

Bearish Signal Reversed

40							X	
		X					X	
		X	O				X	
		X	O	X			B	
		X	O	X	O	X	X	
35		X	O	X	O	X	O	X
			O		O	X	O	X
					O		O	X
							O	
30								

Series of lower tops and higher bottoms. Without period of accumulation, stock reverses the downtrend with a double top buy signal. There must be a minimum of 7 columns to qualify.

Bearish Chart Patterns

Double Bottom

Triple Bottom

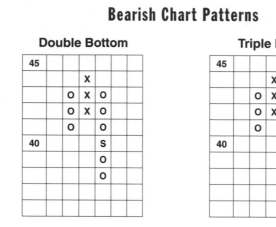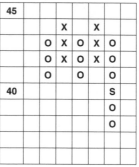

An O (down) column exceeds the previous O (down) column. The simplest of all sell signals.

An O column exceeds two previous columns, or levels of support.

Bearish Catapult

Combination of triple bottom sell signal followed by double bottom sell signal.

Bearish Triangle

Price	1	2	3	4	5
50					
	O				
	O	X			
	O	X	O		
	O	X	O	X	
45	O	X	O	X	O
	O	X	O	X	O
	O	X	O		O
	O				S
					O
40					O

Similar to the bullish triangle, but double bottom is broken to manifest bearish signal. Once again, wait for the double bottom to initiate positions.

Bullish Signal Reversed

Price	1	2	3	4	5	6	7	8	9
40				·					
							X		
							X	O	
						X	X	O	
					X	X	O	X	O
35	O	X	O	X	O	X	O		
	O	X	O	X	O		O		
	O	X	O			S			
	O	X				O			
	O					O			
30						O			

Series of higher tops and higher bottoms. Without a period of distribution, the stock reverses the uptrend with a double bottom sell signal. There must be a minimum of 7 columns to qualify.

and you'll probably quit. The same can happen if you chart too many stocks. Start with twenty to thirty stocks.

Charting by hand will allow you to see reversals take place. It will let you see patterns develop and give you the opportunity to act quickly on those patterns. It will allow you to see if your stocks are rising along with the market or whether there is action contrary to what the market is doing. These contrary actions can often be clues to a change in the stock trend. So don't be afraid to get your hands dirty and chart by hand. ❏

PLAY # 5

Point and Figure Chart Patterns

Professor Herbert Simon, Nobel Laureate, says,
"We need to pay much more explicit attention
to teaching pattern recognition."

SIMON IS KNOWN for his theories about decision making. His studies of the process of chess mastery led to his central finding that pattern recognition is critical. Most would think mastering the game of chess relates to analysis, but Dr. Simon suggests that isn't the case. Success in chess relates to pattern recognition. The more relevant patterns at your disposal, the better your decisions will be.

Just as master chess players excel at pattern recognition on the chess board, accomplished stock market technicians are adept at chart pattern recognition. On pages 16–19 are schematics of the basic chart patterns of the point and figure methodology (**BULLISH CHART PATTERNS/BEARISH CHART PATTERNS**). Committing these patterns to memory will help to promote your overall success in the game of investing. ❏

Adjusting the Box Size on a Point and Figure Chart

The emergence of higher-priced and more volatile stocks
in the late 1990s has made it important to view point
and figure charts with a variety of different box sizes.
This gives the chartist the ability to more easily
see significant areas of support and resistance.

POINT AND FIGURE CHARTS PLOT the price action of a stock. The goal of the chart is to provide an orderly pattern clearly depicting the times that demand and supply are in control. A chart that moves repeatedly from buy to sell signal without showing a clear trend is of little use. Since time is not a consideration when charting, the amount of activity depicted on the chart is based on the price scale, which is located on the vertical axis. The standard scale adjusts as the price of the stock moves higher. The breakpoints are:

¼ point per box from $0 to $5
½ point per box from $5 to $20
1 point per box from $20 to $100
2 points per box from $100 to $200
4 points per box above $200

These changes are not based on percentages; however, the adjustments in scale help account for the larger price movements found in higher-priced stocks. Sometimes we find stocks, as well as whole sectors, that experience wider and wilder price swings. A recent example of this is the Internet stocks. With these stocks it is not uncommon to see 10-point intraday swings. This wild price action causes the chart pattern to become disorderly. The charting analyst begins to see more and more signals, and it becomes increasingly difficult to determine whether demand or supply is in control.

Yahoo! (YHOO): 2 Points Per Box (Standard Size Chart)

	1	2	3	4	5	6	7	8	9	10	11	12	13	14	15	16	17	18
248			X															
244			X	O														
240			X	O														
236			X	O														
232			X	O														
228			X	O														
224	X		X	O	X													
220	X	O	1	O	X	O												
216	X	O	X	O	X	O												
212	X	O	X	O	X	O												
208	X	O		O	X	O												
204	X			O	X	O												
200	X			O	X	O												
198				O	X	O												
196				O	X	O												
194				O	X	O												
192				O	X	O												
190				O	X	O												
188				O	X	O							X					
186				O	X	O					X		X	O				
184				O	X	O		X			X	O	X	O				
182				O		O		X	O		X	O	X	O				
180					O	X		X	O		X	O	X	O				
178					O	X	O	X	O		X	O	X	O				
176					O	X	O	X	O		X	O	X	O				
174					O	X	O	X	O		X	O		O				
172					O	X	O	X	O		X			O				
170					O		O	X	O	X			O	X		X		X
168							O		O	X	O	X	X	O	X	O	X	O
166											O	X	O	X	O	X	O	X
164											O	X	O	X	O	X	O	X
162											O	X	O	X	O	X	O	X
160											O		O	X	O	X	O		X
158											O	2	O	X	O	X		O	X
156											O	X	O		O			O	X
154											O	X	O		O			O	
152											O		O	X					
150													O					
148																		
146																		
144																		
142																		
140																		
138																		
136																		
134																		
132																		
130																		
128																		
126																		
124																		
122																		
120																		
118																		
116																		
114																		
112																		
110																		
108																		

First Quarter 2000
18 buy or sell signals

```
                              X       X
                              X   O   X   O
                              X   O   X   O
                              X   O   X   O
                              X   O   X   O
                              X   O   X   O
                              X   O   X   O
                              X   O       O
                              X           O
          X                   X           O
          X   O   X           X           O
  X       X   O   X   O       X           O
  X   O   X   O   X   O       X           O
  X   O   X   O   X   O   X   X       O   X
  X   O   X   O   X   O   X   O   X       O   X   O
  X   O   X   O   X   O   X   O   X       O   X   O
  X   O   X   O       O   X   O   X       O   X   4   X
  X   O   X   O       O   X   O   X       O   X   O   X   O
O X   O                   O   X   O       O   X   O   X   O
O X                       O   X          O   X   O   X   O
3 X                       O   X          O   X   O   X   O
O X                       O   X              O   X   O
O X                       O                  O   X   O
O X                                          O   X   O
O                                            O   X   O
                                             O   X   O
                                             O   X   O   X
                                             O   X   O   X   O
                                             O   X   O   X   O
                                             O   X   O   X   O
                                             O   X   O   X   O
                                             O   X   O   X   O                   X
                                             O       O   X   O   X               X
                                                     O   O   X   O               X
                                                         O   X   O               X
                                                         O   X   O               X
                                                         O   X   O   X           X
                                                         O   X   O   X   O   X   X
                                                         O   X   O   X   O   X   X
                                                         O   X   O   X   O   X   X
                                                         O   X   O   X   O   X   X
                                                         O   X   O   X   O   X
                                                         O   X   O   X   O
                                                         O   X   O   X
                                                         O   X   O   X
                                                         O   O
```

23

Yahoo! (YHOO): 10 Points Per Box Chart

	1	2	3	4	5	6	7	8
250	X							
240	X	O						
230	1	O						
220	X	O	X					
210	X	O	X	O				
200	X	O	X	O	X			
190	X	O		O	X	O		
180	X			O	3	O		
170	X			O	X	O	X	
160	X			O	X	4	X	O
150	X				2	O	X	O
140	X					O		O
130	X							O
120	C							O
110	X							O
100	B							
90	9							
80	O	X						
70	O	X						
60	8							

First Quarter 2000
3 sell signals on
10-point per box chart

To account for this price action, we often adjust the scale to "slow" the chart down so that it provides an orderly pattern that more clearly identifies whether supply or demand is in control. However, there is a downside to these large-scale charts. It takes a much larger move in the price of the stock to cause the chart to reverse or give a buy or sell signal. When investing in stocks that require these larger box sizes, be sure you can stomach the moves required to form the chart.

Take Yahoo! (YHOO) as an example (**YAHOO! (YHOO): 2 POINTS PER BOX (STANDARD CHART SIZE)**). In the first quarter of 2000 the standard box size chart produced eighteen signals. This wild action proved to be too much. There were eleven sell signals and seven buy signals given in only three months. In order to remove the volatility in the chart, we created a 10-point-per-box and 5-point chart. Remember, the idea is to create an orderly chart pattern that clearly depicts whether supply or demand is in control. By increasing the box size to 10 points, the chart slowed down and produced only three signals during the first quarter of 2000 (**YAHOO! (YHOO): 10 POINTS PER BOX CHART**). More importantly, the signals were consistent. They were all sell signals, along with lower tops. It clearly depicted supply in control. The drawback is that this chart required a 30-point swing just to reverse, which may be too much for many investors to stomach.

If you were looking for more action from the chart, the 5-point chart might have been a better option. It still managed to remove a lot of the whips, as it gave only nine total signals rather than eighteen, and it didn't require such a large move in the stock price to cause a reversal on the chart. Adjusting box sizes is perfectly valid, and when presented with a wild stock, you should use the box size that best fits your investing demeanor. Traders will want to use more active charts (smaller box sizes). Longer-term players will want to find a combination between order and manageable stop-loss points that fits their tolerance. ❑

PLAY # 7

The Bullish Percent Concept

*The bullish percent concept is key to our analysis
of market and industry group sectors.*

THE BULLISH PERCENT concept dates back to the 1940s with Earnest Staby, who noted that market indices were always bullish at the top and bearish at the bottom. He wanted an indicator to show just the opposite. It wasn't until 1955 that A. W. Cohen created the NYSE Bullish Percent to accomplish this goal, that of having an indicator that is bearish at the top and bullish at the bottom (**NYSE BULLISH PERCENT**).

A bullish percent is calculated by dividing the number of stocks that are on a point and figure buy signal within a given universe by the total number of stocks in that universe. For example, if there are 3,000 stocks in the OTC universe and 1,500 are on a point and figure buy signal, the bullish percent reading for the OTC universe would be 50 percent. The resulting percentage is plotted on a grid from 0 percent to 100 percent, much like a football field. Each box on this grid represents 2 percent. Levels above 70 percent are generally considered overbought or high risk, while readings of 30 per-

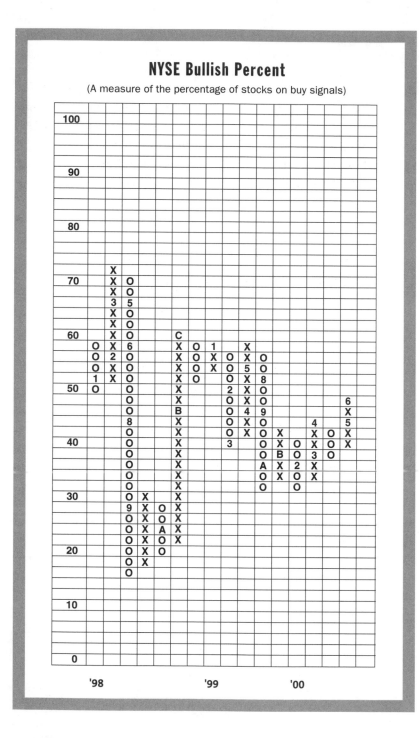

NYSE Bullish Percent

(A measure of the percentage of stocks on buy signals)

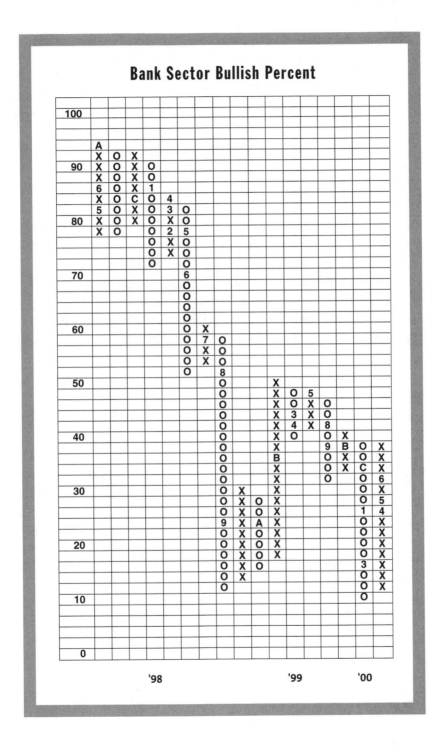

Bank Sector Bullish Percent

cent or lower are considered oversold or low risk. The best buy signals come when a bullish percent goes below 30 percent and then reverses up. Conversely, the best sell signals come when a bullish percent moves above 70 percent and then reverses down and goes below 70 percent. Reversals on a bullish percent chart require a 6 percent change, holding true to the 3-point reversal method. Using the football field analogy, when a bullish percent chart is in Xs, that market or sector is said to be on offense, or having possession of the football. Your enthusiasm is tempered as the field position gets closer to the overbought 70 percent territory. When a bullish percent chart is in Os, that market or sector is said to be on defense, or having lost possession of the football. When the bullish percent dictates that the offensive team is on the field, you are trying to score against the market by employing wealth accumulation strategies. But when the bullish percent dictates that the defense is on the field, the market is trying to score against you; therefore, you must employ wealth preservation strategies (**NYSE BULLISH PERCENT** and **BANK SECTOR BULLISH PERCENT**). ❏

MARKET
PSYCHOLOGY

HAVE YOU EVER HEARD that phrase, "You can be your own worst enemy"? When the football team steps on the field Sunday afternoon, all the players must come with a positive mental attitude, believing they are going to win. Exuding confidence is often the key to success in sports, life, and investing, too. The only way to gain confidence is to be prepared and to control your negative thoughts.

The human traits of greed and fear can get in the way of making sound investment decisions. Intellectually, you may know the right course of action, but when it comes to executing the plan, emotions can get in the way. To complicate matters, the market is not always fair. You can execute the plan correctly, but the outcome is not always what you expected, even if you made the proper decision. The following tips will help you to develop a better psychological edge in competing against the emotional woes of investing.

PLAY #8

Finding a Discipline

Find a methodology that you believe in, one that
meets your risk characteristics and financial goals.
Practice it well and then stick with it.

What Works On Wall Street (O'Shaughnessy, McGraw-Hill, 1998) is an interesting market book because it includes lots of different approaches to making money in the stock market. We've met many different successful traders and investors. Some have used the point and figure methodology as their investment philosophy and some have not. Interestingly enough, those who used the point and figure methodology all applied it a little bit differently. The common thread among all of these investors was their ability to stay focused on their game plan. They established their game plan and then went about executing it. They weren't jumping from one philosophy or methodology to another every six months or every time they had a bad trade.

We look at trading and investment disciplines a lot like athletics. A coach develops plays, let's say in basketball, based on the players' talent levels and skills. He teaches those plays every day until the team can run them in their sleep. Just because they lose a game doesn't mean they start the next practice with a new set of plays. Consistently playing your game over time simply leads to more wins than attempting new plays every week.

Imagine having to learn a new way of investing every six months!

In order for investors to be consistent with a particular investment discipline, it needs to be flexible enough to operate in bullish, bearish, and neutral markets. It must be adaptable enough to signal up-and-coming market leaders and market laggards. It needs to provide not only a buy strategy, but also a sell strategy, since capital preservation is just as important as capital appreciation.

We have an unwavering belief in the point and figure methodology. Point and figure is rooted in the core economic theory of supply and demand. No matter what new technology and industries come along and which ones fade out, supply and demand controls them, and that shows up in the chart patterns. The chart patterns and relative strength also provide for a buy and sell strategy.

Tom Landry, the NFL defensive back and coach, perfectly captures our philosophy on discipline: "Setting a goal is not the main thing. It is deciding how you will go about achieving it and staying with that plan. The key is discipline." ❑

PLAY #9

Common Investor Mistakes

Below we have listed a few common investor mistakes.
Try to avoid making these mistakes with your investments.

◆ **Falling in love with a position.** An account has limited capital, so ask yourself if the position is the best one to be in here. Are you tying up capital that can be put to better use elsewhere? Don't get sucked into the fundamental story—that is, don't hold on to a stock whose technical picture has deteriorated just because you are intoxicated with the reasons for your choice.

◆ **Buying the stock right, but forgetting to sell it right.** There are two foul shots to make successfully with respect to investing. You must buy the stock right, and then you must sell the stock correctly. Therefore, once you buy a stock you must review it on a regular basis; don't just forget about it. Attempt to sink both foul shots.

◆ **Not having a game plan for investing.** Investors will haphazardly, especially in a strong market, pick stocks to buy, thinking that the stock market is easy to beat. They fail to realize there is risk, not only reward. Therefore, it is essential to have a game plan that helps dictate what stocks to buy and when, and also tells you when to sell or play defense.

◆ **Buying stocks that are extended.** When you buy a stock that is up on a stem, it increases your risk and diminishes your potential reward. Rather, it is best to buy a stock when it pulls back closer to support, thereby increasing the potential upside reward, and diminishing the risk to the stop-loss point.

◆ **Taking small gains, but not being willing to take small losses.** Be willing to take small losses by adhering to your stop-loss points. Avoiding large losses will keep you in the game. You will not be right on every trade, so be willing to bail out and take the small loss when the technical picture so dictates.

◆ **Buying a stock that is trending down, thinking that it is cheap, or a value.** Often, these types of stocks become an even better value because they continue to fall in price. Ideally, it is best to stick to stocks that are in an overall uptrend, trading above their bullish support line and exhibiting positive relative strength. These are the stocks that are in demand and should be considered for purchase.

◆ **Acting on poor advice, tips, and financial media hype.** Many investors try to get rich quick without doing their homework. They rely on the TV or financial media to tell them what to buy. Instead, take the time to educate yourself, to arm yourself with a game plan. Then you will be able to make sound, informed decisions. Take responsibility for your own success. Don't rely on get-rich-quick schemes and rumors. Do your own research.

◆ **Getting emotional and not being able to stay objective.** Any investor knows that emotions can be your worst enemy. Try to stay objective. The point and figure chart helps you accomplish this because a picture paints a thousand words. When looking at the chart, cover up the name of the stock. Make your decision on what the chart is telling you, therefore taking the emotion out of knowing the name of the stock. ❏

Ten Ways to Sabotage Your Portfolio

This is a great tongue-in-cheek presentation of what not to do to keep your investments healthy. This humorous presentation comes to us courtesy of DWA's money managers Mike Moody and Harold Parker.

1 Be arrogant. The market teaches humility. As soon as you believe you know why the market acts, you will be proven wrong. Arrogance can kill a portfolio. You must be able to admit defeat and preserve enough capital to fight again. Following the point and figure charts, which depict the battle between supply and demand, helps keep you out of the "I know why" attitude of investing.

2 When a sector reverses up, wait until you feel comfortable to buy. Falling into this trap is a great way to ensure that you buy the stock at a higher price. We use the bullish percent indicators to track the risk in sectors. These indicators are soulless. In other words, they are not emotional and do not get caught up in recent news events and common thinking. When sectors reverse up from oversold levels, it is often when the news is the most dire. Conventional wisdom would suggest this is the last place in the world you would want to invest. Buying at this time is gut wrenching, but to be successful you must have complete confidence in the indicator. As the sector moves higher, the comfort level increases. If you use comfort level as your guidance, however, you will for sure leave a lot of money on the table, or worse, buy as the sector peaks.

3 Be afraid to buy strong stocks. Do this to make sure you stay out of the long-term winners. Don't avoid stocks just because they have gone up. Doing this will keep you out of the leaders. This mentality would have kept you out of General Electric (GE), which was up 188 percent between January 1995 and December 1997 only to see it rally another 96 percent by the end of 2000. It also would have kept you out of Cisco (CSCO), which was up 376 percent between January 1995 and December 1997, and then it moved up another 312 percent by the end of 2000. These are only two examples, but there are many others.

More important than how much the stock is up is its supply and demand relationship. By evaluating the point and figure chart, you can gain insight into this relationship and whether or not the stock is likely to move higher. Stocks that double can easily double again. Don't miss out on these great opportunities.

4 Sell a stock because it has gone up. Doing this cuts profits short. Buying a stock right is only half the battle. You have to be able to sell it right to win the war. Just because a stock has rallied 30 percent or 50 percent, don't be tempted to take your trade off for that reason alone. Consider trimming the position and leave part on the table to continue in the uptrend. Let profits run.

5 Buy stocks in sectors that are extended because it's different this time. On the surface, the stock market appears different all the time. The leadership changes: in come the Nifty 50, and then out they go. Small-cap stocks outperform for a while, then it's back to the large caps. However, the underlying forces that drive the stock market are always the same. They are true and time-tested and do not change. They are supply and demand. That's why buying sectors that are extended (overbought) will not be different this time.

6 Try to bottom fish a stock in a downtrend. "The trend is your friend" is a true statement. So don't go against it without some inkling that the trend has changed. Bottom fishing a stock in a downtrend is the opposite of being afraid to buy strong stocks. Do not buy a stock just because it fell sharply. You want to buy a stock that is likely to move higher, not one that is not likely to fall further.

At a minimum, wait for the stock to show a sign that demand is back in control and suggesting higher prices. That may be a simple buy signal on the chart or a reversal back to the upside after holding an area of support. Also remember why you initiated the position. Be careful not to let a trade turn into something else.

7 Buy a stock because it is a good value. These days, value is in the eyes of the holder, and therefore it is a subjective term at best. If a stock has become a good value, ask why. This is important, because a stock can stay a good value by not moving for the next decade, or worse, become a better value by dropping another 20 percent.

The true value of a stock is determined by its capital appreciation potential, not numbers on a balance sheet. The basis for capital appreciation lies in the supply and demand relationship of the stock. Appreciation can occur only if demand grows stronger for the stock and buyers are willing to pay a higher price. Watch the point and figure charts to determine if a stock is likely to move higher in price and become a good value.

8 Hold on to losing stocks and hope they come back. Hope is eternal, but your portfolio is not. Holding on to a losing stock is the best way to let your losses run. Combine this mistake with selling a stock that has gone up and you can create a portfolio of dogs.

When buying stocks, there will always be some losers: Count on it. However, how you manage that loss often determines the success or failure of the overall portfolio. Keep losses small so that you have the capital to play again. Hanging on to losing positions, hoping that they will come back, can be deadly. A $50 stock that is stopped out at $40 is a 20 percent loss. It's a bad trade, but it is manageable. In order to recoup that loss you would have to make 25 percent on a $40 stock. What if you held on to that $50 stock, hoping that strong earnings would come in and turn it around, but instead it continued lower to $25? Finally, you decide to exit, but now it takes a 100 percent return from a $25 stock just to get back to even. Those results are hard to find, and if you are able to find one, you don't want to waste it on getting back to even.

Learn to recognize your losing positions for what they are. If a stock cannot trade above its support line or is not outperforming the averages, find one that is and swap it.

9 Pursue perfection. There are two types of mistakes to discuss here. The first is the constant belief that there is a better system out there, and you need to find it. Using a new system to invest each week will not get you to your goal. You will become good at nothing and moderate to bad at everything. To be good requires that you stay focused, disciplined, and skilled at whatever methodology you choose. You need to have the strength of conviction in your chosen discipline to learn from mistakes rather than to run away from them and find another methodology. There is no Holy Grail in investing.

The second mistake is to wait for the perfect trade. There is no such thing. If you only buy stocks that have all positive attributes you will maintain a portfolio of cash. Rarely, if ever, do you find a stock that has all the pluses on its side. Look for the big ones like relative strength, trend, and signal. Also remember that 80 percent of the cause of price movement in a stock is based on the market and sector. You are better off being approximately right than precisely wrong.

10 Do anything based on a magazine cover. Following the hot news that appears on magazine covers is a shortcut to the poorhouse. Why should you follow the advice of someone who has just moved from the society pages to the business section? ❏

PLAY # 11

Our Adaptation of Baruch's Rules

Bernard M. Baruch, famed Wall Street financier and statesman, had his own guidelines for investing or speculating in the stock market. We suggest that you, too, adhere to rules or a game plan when investing. There is a time to buy and a time to sell, and you must know when that time is.

BARUCH SAYS IN *My Own Story* (Buccaneer Books, 1997) that his rules reflect two lessons that experience has taught him: "that getting the facts of a situation before acting is of crucial importance, and that getting these facts is a continuous job, which requires eternal vigilance." We couldn't agree more with Mr. Baruch.

To us, "getting the facts of the situation first" means consulting the point and figure chart. This chart acts as your road map, directing the course you should take with the given stock. The chart answers the technical side of the equation—if or when the trip should be taken. Baruch then states that this is a continuous job. Once you embark on your investment trip, you must continually consult that road map—the point and figure chart. You must make the trip there, then use the map to get back home. Or said another way, you must review the stock position constantly, because the chart is evolving and changing over time; this is all in an effort to buy the stock right, then sell it right. The chart will help make your round trip a successful one. ❏

Practice, Practice, and Then Practice Some More

The market doesn't wait around for you to catch up.
It is a moving target, and when situations change, you must
know instinctively what your next move is going to be.

"Discipline is a part of the will. A disciplined person is one who follows the will of the one who gives the orders. You teach discipline by doing it over and over, by repetition and rote, especially in a game like football where you have very little time to decide what you are going to do. So what you do is react almost instinctively, naturally. You have done it so many times, over and over and over again."

VINCE LOMBARDI, NFL COACH AND GENERAL MANAGER

MANY COMPARISONS CAN BE made between the stock market and sports. Most parents want their child to be involved in some type of sport, from baseball to basketball to football to swimming to dance. It is because sports teach us valuable lessons that we carry throughout life. Participation in sports teaches us about commitment, hard work, the value of teamwork, wanting to excel, the thrill of victory, learning to accept defeat, sportsmanship in victory and defeat, and the importance of practice. Very few people are born with the natural instinct to hit a baseball or throw a football. Some may be born with a body built for being a defensive lineman, for example, but the actual skills have to be learned. To be learned well, those skills must be practiced over and over again.

When it comes to making a decision in the market, it's very much like a football game. As the quarterback, the ball's been snapped, it's in your hands, and now you have to try to make forward progress. You have a split second to decide whether you're going to throw the ball, hand it off, or carry it yourself. So what you do is react almost instinctively, as Vince Lombardi says. You have been to practice so many times that when you step back and take a look at the defense as it is coming at you, you instinctively know what the defense is and you react.

The markets are the same way. The market is coming at you (trying to take your money away from you). You don't have long to look at the position of the players on the field and decide what type of play you want to run. Do you throw the long pass (like what you would do when the bullish percent is just reversing up from below 30 percent)? Do you give it to the fullback and try to inch up the field (when the bullish percent is at 68 percent and approaching the red zone)?

The markets move so much faster today than ten years ago or even five years ago (especially for the short-term trader) that these moves have to be instinctual. If a stock completes a bearish catapult formation and violates its bullish support line you should instinctively know you must implement some type of defensive strategy.

The only way you are going to know how to instinctively implement your game plan is by practice. Practice looking at different chart patterns and analyzing what happened afterwards. If you look at enough bearish catapults, you will develop an understanding that this pattern usually leads to lower prices. Look at enough bullish triangle patterns and it becomes instinct that stocks usually see a nice trading pop after the breakout. Look at enough sectors above 70 percent and you'll learn that it is an extremely risky time to be buying, as stocks almost always can be bought later at better prices. Make flash cards of the patterns; take fifteen minutes each day and study a stock's historical chart; devote a weekend to looking at sector bullish percent charts; and do practice case studies, so that when the time comes to make a decision, you're ready. ❏

PLAY # 13

Why Work with a Broker or Money Manager?

While we endeavor to teach investors and brokers how to manage their own money, there are circumstances that make it worthwhile to consider using the services of a money manager.

WE'VE ALL SEEN those commercials by the online brokerage services that bash the stockbroker. You know which ones I'm talking about. The guy is washing his boat and says, "The only thing my broker did was make me broker." Or the award-winning commercial with the truck driver who has a picture of his island on the dashboard. While these commercials get our attention, make us laugh, and get us to wonder if it is that easy, they do make you think about what value the full-service financial adviser or money manager should provide. Here are just some of the benefits we see in dealing with a professional who has a solid game plan for investing.

◆ Personalized service instead of using the bandwagon approach, i.e., "What's best for the masses must be best for me, too."

◆ Keeping you on track with the game plan. When the temptation to jump is the greatest because you have that feeling of "if I don't buy now I'm going to miss out," your stockbroker can gently remind you of the sector field position at 90 percent. At 30 percent, when you should be buying, you may feel your stomach churning, but this is when your investment adviser can counsel you through difficult market environments because he's been there before. He's seen 30 percent, 70 percent, and everything in between.

◆ The point and figure methodology is something you and your broker can work on together. For instance, he can e-mail you charts. You still stay informed and involved in the process, but don't have to do the day-to-day portfolio maintenance.

◆ As a busy professional yourself, you may not have the time to devote to your investments that they require. For instance, we can book our own flights on the Internet, but we still use our travel agency because it provides a valuable service. Our associates could spend forty-five minutes on the Internet looking up everything and booking it, but their time is better spent doing point and figure research. In a five-minute phone call, they can give our travel agent the details of when and where they're going, and the travel agent takes care of the rest.

◆ What about the rest of your family? Maybe you really take a keen interest in the stock market and understanding how to pick stocks, but your spouse might not share that same enthusiasm. When preparing for the future, wouldn't it be a good idea to have someone who enthusiastically understands your financial picture and your goals? If Noah had waited until he felt a raindrop to start building the ark, then he would not have been ready for the flood. Don't wait until a crisis arises to take action. Do your homework and make plans ahead of time so that when the need arises, the transition is much easier. ❏

PLAY # 14

Decision Doesn't Dictate Outcome— Use the Tools Properly: That's the Best You Can Do

When you make a decision to buy a stock, you have to realize that the outcome is independent of the decision. That is, you don't always achieve the outcome you would like—that of making money. But over time, if you use the point and figure tools properly, you will likely have more positive outcomes than negative.

IN INVESTING, YOU MUST realize that nothing is a guarantee. The best you can do is stack the odds of success in your favor, make the proper decision according to what your investment tools are telling you, and then wait for the outcome. The point and figure methodology we employ is designed to improve these probabilities of success in investing by helping you make a sound decision.

Unfortunately, this investment game is not always accommodating. There are times when you make the proper decision, but don't get the outcome that you had anticipated. Does that mean you were wrong? No. Not every trade is always going to work out exactly as you have planned. You will have times when a stock will go against you for any number of unforeseen reasons. That is life on Wall Street. But investors falsely believe that if a trade doesn't work out, you made a bad decision. That's wrong. Therefore, it is imperative to educate yourself. Be sure you understand the game plan and know why you are making certain decisions. If you know you used the tools correctly, you will be able to accept the outcome, good or bad.

To illustrate how the "decision" should be looked upon as separate from the "outcome," let's look at the following scenario:

Take a coin with both heads and tails. If the coin is tossed and heads comes up, you will be paid $1.25. If the coin is tossed and tails comes up, you will be paid $1.00. Shouldn't you always bet on heads?

Fifty percent of the time heads will come up and you will be a winner, and 50 percent of the time tails will come up and you will be a loser, but over time you will make more money because you are paid more for the heads.

So the point is, if your investment research tools tell you to make a certain decision based on the information you have at the time, make that decision. Over time, since these tools are designed to increase your odds of success, you will be a winner. ❏

PLAY # 15

Magazine Covers

Don't believe everything you read.

YOU MAY HAVE A wonderful market indicator right in your own home. The magazines you have around the house can be a very good way to get information on the market, as long as you program yourself to do the opposite of what the cover implies. This may sound harsh to some of you. It is not meant to be. That is just the way it is, especially if the magazine in question is a non-financial publication. We have seen *Playboy* give mutual fund advice on how to pick winners. When the market is so good and so strong that a magazine like *Playboy* is giving investment advice, you know it is time to be careful.

This is true at market tops and market bottoms. When the market declined strongly in 1998, many people wondered if the long-running bull market was over. *Time* featured a cover in September 1998 with the title "Is the Boom Over?," while *Newsweek*'s cover during the same period was "The Crash of '99" (in anticipation of a possible crash the following year).

This phenomenon is not exclusive to such magazines as *Time* and *Newsweek*. Business periodicals do the same thing. *Fortune* showed a cover in September 1998 proclaiming "The Crash of '98: Can the U.S. Economy Hold Up?" while *Forbes* asked, "Is It Armageddon?" You get the idea. Here are four different publications, two business related and two not, and all of their covers are on the market and all are wondering if the end is near.

Of course it wasn't. The market rallied strongly after that, and no doubt the editors quickly forgot these covers. What you want to keep in mind is that these covers appear more often than not once the bad news is out. If the market declines 1 percent or 2 percent from the highs, that is not a story significant enough for the cover of a magazine. We must fall a great deal, enough to get everyone's attention, in order to make the cover. And once it has everyone's focus, it is often the wrong time for you, the investor, to take action, unless that action is in the opposite direction. Remember, the job of the journalist is to report on what is happening *today,* but as investors, we want to focus on what is going to happen in the future.

As another example, on the day after the October 19th crash in 1987, the *New York Times* had a headline asking if 1987 equals 1929. As you already know, the answer to this question was no, and had you purchased stocks in the aftermath of that major decline in the market in 1987, you did extremely well.

You may ask if this was true for individual stocks, and for the most part, the answer was yes. In 1999, *Forbes* named Pfizer its stock of the year. It was down for the year. After notable declines on two separate occasions, McDonald's was featured in a negative light on the cover of *BusinessWeek* magazine. If you bought the stock a couple of weeks after these magazines hit the newsstands, you did very well. This is not a foolproof method, but it can be a useful tool for you. The next time you are in the grocery line waiting to check out, you may want to take a peek at the magazine covers. You may just pay for those groceries with a trade. ❏

A Diary of Lessons

Keep a diary of the trades you make, and then once you close out a trade, go back and objectively review the whole position from beginning to end. Seeing what you did right and what you did wrong will make you a better trader or investor for the future.

WHEN THE BOTTOM falls out of the market and investors begin losing money, they often take on a school-age mentality and begin pointing the finger at their peers. "It's his fault!" They look to the Fed, market gurus who lower their equity ratings, online trading, chat rooms, margin calls, Asian Flu, etc. During any market cycle, the best thing one can do is ask, "What can I learn from this situation?"

The best traders and investors always evaluate what went right and what went wrong in their trades. Look at how you handled the downturn in the market and see what you did right and what you did wrong. Consider the following:

◆ Did you initiate new positions when the sector was at 90 percent?

◆ Did you fall in love with your stocks and forget they don't love you back?

◆ Did you abandon the game plan because "it's different this time"?

◆ Did you own stocks in which the volatility was OK on the upside but not on the downside?

◆ Did you decide to disregard the chart pattern and the sell signals?

◆ Did you say, "I'm a long-term investor" until your stock was down 50 percent?

◆ Did you initiate the buy portion of the trade correctly but not the sell side?

◆ Did you let your clients or friends sway you from your game plan?

◆ Did you hold onto a dead horse, lighting candles and hoping for a miracle cure?

◆ Did you heed the sell signals, so that your account then had cash available at the bottom?

◆ Did you take partial positions off the table, lessening the blow?

◆ Did you switch some of your holdings into defensive issues?

These are just some of the questions to ask yourself. The market is a continuing learning process, and we're never too old to learn. Take time to sit down and evaluate how you handled the last market cycle, and be honest with yourself. When things don't go our way, it is always easiest to look for someone else to blame rather than looking to ourselves for what we might have done wrong.

And in some cases, you didn't do anything wrong. Sometimes you do everything exactly right, given the information at the time, and the trade doesn't work out. That's life on Wall Street. Nothing is ever 100 percent correct. And remember, if you did the right thing and raised cash before a market downturn, holding only those stocks with strong relative strength, but your portfolio still gave back some headway, that's OK. It's a big bet to go to 100 percent cash, but you are sitting better than a lot of people and have cash available to employ on the next opportunity. If you did gravitate from the game plan, use this evaluation process as a wake-up call to reacquaint yourself with your plan. Learn from the experience, so that the next time a high-risk situation presents itself (and you can rest assured it will), you will be ready to take action. If you ignore your mistakes, you will just keep making them over and over again. ❑

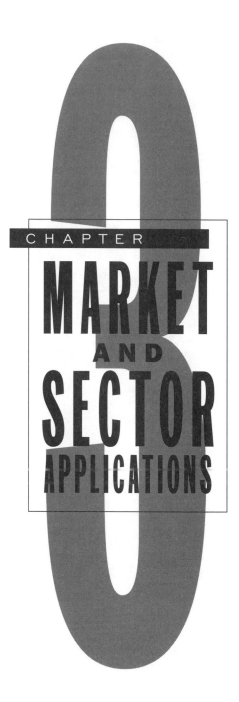

CHAPTER

MARKET
AND
SECTOR
APPLICATIONS

IN CHAPTER 1 WE DISCUSSED the importance of having a game plan and a playbook for investing. It is also important to know what stadium you are playing in and what time the game starts. For instance, a football player would not show up at the swimming pool, nor would a golfer tee up the ball on a baseball field. In other words, each sport has its own playing field. The same is true in investing. The following tips will educate you on some of the intricacies of market index composition and weighting, sector timing, and sector-relative strength. Or said another way, they will let you know what stadium your game is in and if the playing field is level.

Once you know the stadium you're playing in, the football game starts with a coin toss. This determines who will get possession of the football first, or said another way, whose offensive team will start the game. We use a top-down approach to investing; that is, we analyze the market and sector risk first, before moving to the stock itself. This is the point at which in our game plan we determine whether you as an investor should be playing offense or defense. Just as the quarterback sits on the bench when the opposition has the ball, there are times when it is in your best interest as an investor to sit on the sidelines. These tips will teach you the benefits of placing great focus on your market and sector analysis in an attempt to score against your opponent, the stock market.

PLAY # 1 7

The 80 Percent–20 Percent Phenomenon

The cause of price movement in any given stock is predominantly a function of market and sector risk. More specifically, 80 percent of the risk in any given stock is attributable to the market and sector. Yet the typical time allocation for researching a stock is 80 percent to the actual stock and only 20 percent to the market and sector.

IN THE GRAPH SHOWN AT RIGHT, you can see that 31 percent of the risk in a given stock is a function of the market risk, 49 percent a function of the sector risk, and only 20 percent is attributable to the stock itself. But as you can see, the majority of time and resources (80 percent) are allocated to the company itself—or to the specific fundamentals of that company.

This study by the University of Chicago plainly points out the need for technical analysis. The fundamental analyst is looking at only 20 percent of the pie! Fundamental analysts are just trying to pick out the best stock in their group. But they are not telling you

SOURCES: *THE NEW SCIENCE OF INVESTING* BY DR. ROBERT HAGEN, AND *THE LATENT STATISTICAL STRUCTURE OF SECURITIES PRICE CHANGES*, BY BENJAMIN KING.

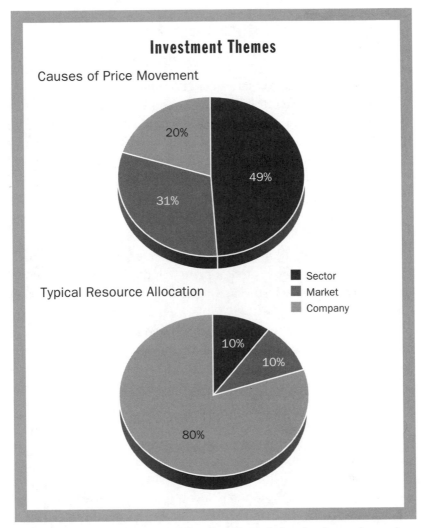

if their group is going to perform well, and that is where the majority of risk lies. Therefore, you must use the fundamentals to tell you what to buy, and you must use the technical picture to tell you when to buy.

There are times when the market or a given sector dictates defense. And just as vegetables go in and out of season, so do sectors. So when evaluating a given stock, be sure to first determine if the market and its given sector suggest a bullish environment (INVESTMENT THEMES). ❑

Why the S&P 500 Is Hard to Beat

Investors tend to compare their portfolio's return to that of the S&P 500 (SPX). This isn't necessarily a fair comparison. Why? The SPX, on the surface, appears to be a well-balanced basket of 500 stocks, but in fact, because it is a capitalization-weighted index, this is not the case. The effects of market capitalization therefore make it very difficult to beat the S&P 500, and suggest you should compare your well-diversified portfolio's return to a more representative market index.

THE S&P 500 IS A capitalization or market-weighted index rather than an equal-weighted or price-weighted index. This means that the SPX gives each stock a weight in proportion to the market cap of the company. As an example, General Electric (GE) is the largest company in the United States based on market capitalization, so it has the biggest weighting in the S&P 500 (currently 4.33 percent). Even though there are 500 stocks in the index, the overall movement of the SPX will be more heavily influenced by only a few stocks, those with the largest market caps.

GE accounts for 4.33 percent of the S&P 500 index, while Super-Valu (SVU), holding slot number 400 in market cap, constitutes only .025 percent. As a result, GE's impact on the performance of the SPX is more than 170 times that of SVU. Therefore, because of its weightings, the S&P 500 is much more narrowly focused on the large-cap stocks, oftentimes unbeknownst to the average investor. For example, in 1999 the SPX was up 21 percent for the year. Ten stocks accounted for almost 65 percent of that gain! You better have owned those ten stocks if you expected to be anywhere close to outperforming the index. To boot, if you unweighted the S&P 500, it was only up a little more than 3 percent in 1999.

The effect of weighting, therefore, makes it difficult to outperform the SPX if you employ an equally weighted, well-diversified investment strategy (and we haven't even discussed the impact of commissions or fees). The only way to do so is to focus on just a few names, but at what risk? Better to do the right thing: follow your game plan, diversify, and manage the portfolio. Then at a minimum, compare yourself to the unweighted SPX, or some other broad, equal-weighted index. It's only fair. ❏

Bogey Fever

Our money managers, like other investment managers and brokers, fight a constant battle with investors about realistic benchmarks for performance. The bogey that is chosen can make you and/or the managers you recommended for your client a hero or a zero, so correct selection is important.

INVESTORS USUALLY WANT the bogey to be whatever index had the most spectacular performance over the past twelve months. If their small-cap manager beat their small-cap benchmark, they want to know why they didn't beat the S&P 500. If their large-cap manager beat the S&P 500, they want to know why they didn't beat the Nasdaq 100 or the Internet Index. If investors focus only on performance, they miss the point of the benchmarks in the first place: to assess manager skill. The whole point of a bogey is to determine whether the manager is adding value or not.

The Association of Investment Management and Research (AIMR) has published the most comprehensive guidelines on performance reporting. Their general position is that the benchmark should match the type of securities in the account and the way the portfolio is constructed. Obviously, it makes no sense to benchmark an international manager against the Dow Jones, which is a domestic index. But that's the easy part.

The tricky part comes when you start to look at how the portfolio is constructed. Many common benchmarks are capitalization-weighted, but many investment managers run equal-weighted portfolios, in which each position might be 3 percent of the account, for instance. The differences between them can be dramatic.

For example, many large-cap managers use the S&P 500 as a bogey. This would be absolutely reasonable if they ran a capitalization-weighted account. The Vanguard Index 500 Fund, for instance, *is* cap-weighted, and *should* be compared to a cap-weighted index to see if any value is being added. But a large-cap manager running an equal-weighted account should be benchmarked against something like the S&P 500 Unweighted Geometric, which had a 1999 performance of +3.06 percent, rather than the +21.04 percent return of the cap-weighted version. Keep in mind that the eighteen percentage points of difference reflect the performance of exactly the same 500 stocks, just weighted differently. If managers can tack on performance above the benchmark, they are adding value within their selection universe and showing some evidence of skill. A manager could reasonably be compared to the S&P SuperComposite 1500, which is cap-weighted and returned 20.26 percent for 1999, or to the Value Line Geometric, which is equal-weighted and was down 1.40 percent for the year, depending on how the portfolio is constructed.

Finally, once you have the proper bogey, you need sufficient time to assess manager skill. One year, clearly, is not enough. Clocking Frank Shorter's 100-meter time will not tell you anything about his ability to run a marathon. Statistically, thirty years would be nice to establish significance, but most investors are not likely to be that patient! The happy medium might be three, five, or ten years, depending on the investor's style. ❏

PLAY #20

Do You Know Your QQQs?

If used correctly, index-based products can provide your account with great diversification.

THE PROLIFERATION OF index-based products has provided us with great investment vehicles offering instant diversification. Some excellent examples are the S&P 500 SPDRs, the Dow Diamonds (DIA), and the Nasdaq 100 Trust (QQQ). However, a word to the wise: the diversification in these index-based products can be misleading. The Nasdaq 100 Trust comprises 100 stocks, so you might think you are receiving the diversification of 100 issues.

That's not the case. The Nasdaq 100 is a capitalization-weighted index, and therefore, some stocks are more important in calculating the index than others. In fact, as we are writing this, the top ten stocks in the QQQ account for 43.487 percent of the movement of the Nasdaq 100, and the top twenty stocks account for 60.221 percent of the movement in the Nasdaq 100. That means when you purchase the QQQs you are essentially purchasing a basket of ten to twenty stocks, not 100 stocks. Purchasing a basket of ten technology stocks is a great way to play the technology movement, but you must be aware of exactly what you are purchasing so that you can accurately evaluate the position.

To illustrate the point, let's look at the OTC Bullish Percent and the QQQs. The OTC Bullish Percent is an equally weighted index, since each stock gets one vote. It doesn't matter that some stocks have a bigger capitalization weighting. Each stock gets treated the same. However, in the QQQ, the bigger the company, the more votes it gets. So if you try to trade the Nasdaq 100 based on the OTC Bullish Percent, your results may or may not be successful. Using the OTC Bullish Percent to trade the QQQs is like comparing apples to oranges. A much better way to evaluate it is to examine very closely the top ten stocks comprising the index. These are the primary stocks that influence the price movement, so their performance will dictate the performance of the index. For instance, if the OTC Bullish Percent drops to 20 percent, but the top twenty-five capitalized stocks in the OTC market remain unchanged in price, then the QQQs would barely budge on the downside.

Remember, an OTC Bullish Percent reading of 16 percent would mean 16 percent of the stocks remained on buy signals. A better way to evaluate the QQQ is to look at a technical picture of the top ten capitalized stocks in the index.

Let's look at another example showing why it is important to evaluate what is moving these indices. Microsoft accounts for about 7 percent of the Nasdaq 100 Trust index. So let's say you were thinking about buying the QQQ and also taking a big position in Microsoft. After realizing that Microsoft has a big influence on the index, you might decide to diversify with other software stocks. In fact, did you know that when you look at the Nasdaq Composite, Dow Jones, and

S&P 500, there are essentially thirty-one stocks that move 50 percent of each of these indices? Therefore, when you hear the popular financial news media talk about the market being up or down, keep in mind that they are talking about just thirty-one stocks!

Below is a quick review of the Nasdaq 100 Trust, S&P 500 SPDRs (SPY), and Dow Jones Diamonds (DIA), and the component influence as of April 30, 2000. A great Web site for more information on many of these products is the American Stock Exchange at www.amex.com.

NASDAQ 100 TRUST (QQQ)

THIS TRUST REPRESENTS the largest and most active nonfinancial domestic and international issues listed on the Nasdaq stock market based on market capitalization. The composition is reviewed quarterly and adjustments are made as necessary.

As of this writing, the ten largest holdings account for 43 percent of the index's movement, while the top twenty names account for 60 percent of the index's movement. At right are the top twenty stocks in the QQQ, listed in descending order of the percent of the index they comprise (NASDAQ 100 TRUST TOP TWENTY NAMES).

SPDRs (SPY)

STANDARD & POOR'S DEPOSITARY RECEIPTS are based on the S&P 500 Composite Stock Price Index. The SPY is essentially one-tenth the price of the S&P 500 Index. The SPY can also pay quarterly cash dividends representing dividends accumulated on the stocks of the S&P 500, less fees and expenses of the trust.

The top ten capitalized stocks in the S&P 500 account for 25 percent of that index's movement. In a capitalization-weighted index, the larger the capitalization, the more influence the stock has. In other words, Microsoft gets more votes than Citigroup. On page 58 is a listing of the top twenty capitalized stocks on the SPY. The top twenty stocks in the SPY account for 39 percent of the movement of the index. Or, said another way, 4 percent of the stocks in the index carry 39 percent of the weighting (S&P 500 TOP TWENTY CAPITALIZED STOCKS).

Nasdaq 100 Trust Top Twenty Names

As of April 2000

STOCK	SYMBOL	WEIGHTING (AS OF 4/2000)
Intel	INTC	7.461%
Cisco Systems	CSCO	7.414
Microsoft	MSFT	6.887
JDS Uniphase	JDSU	5.159
Oracle	ORCL	4.131
Sun Microsystems	SUNW	2.875
Nextel Comm-A	NXTL	2.610
Qualcomm	QCOM	2.561
Worldcom	WCOM	2.243
Dell Computer	DELL	2.146
Veritas Software	VRTS	2.098
Immunex	IMNX	1.856
Siebel Systems	SEBL	1.855
Amgen	AMGN	1.691
Applied Materials	AMAT	1.667
ADC Telecom	ADCT	1.643
Xilinx	XLNX	1.599
Yahoo	YHOO	1.524
Verisign	VRSN	1.487
Ciena	CIEN	1.314

DOW JONES DIAMONDS (DIA)

ON JANUARY 20, 1998, the Dow Jones DIAMONDS (DIA) started trading. This security allows investors to buy and sell shares on an entire portfolio of Dow Jones stocks.

The DJIA is a price-weighted index and not a capitalization-weighted index. In a price-weighted index, the higher the stock price, the more effect it has on the average. For instance, let's say Intel (INTC) and Walt Disney (DIS) both rallied 10 percent. For Intel, that would be 13.2 points, and for Disney it would be 3.8

S&P 500 Top Twenty Capitalized Stocks

As of April 2000

STOCK	SYMBOL	WEIGHTING (AS OF 4/2000)
General Electric	GE	3.993%
Intel	INTC	3.556
Cisco Systems	CSCO	3.449
Microsoft	MSFT	3.340
Pfizer	PFE	2.395
Exxon Mobil	XON	2.157
Wal-Mart	WMT	2.031
Citigroup	C	1.721
Nortel Networks	NT	1.684
Oracle	ORCL	1.654
American International Group	AIG	1.488
Lucent Technologies	LU	1.473
International Business Machines	IBM	1.439
Merck & Co.	MRK	1.417
EMC Corp.	EMC	1.307
SBC Communications	SBC	1.245
Verizon Communications	VZ	1.208
Coca-Cola	KO	1.166
Johnson & Johnson	JNJ	1.124
Sun Microsystems	SUNW	1.102

SOURCE: BLOOMBERG L.P.

points. Intel would add 74.66 points to the DJIA, but Disney, only 21.49 points. The ten highest-priced stocks in the Dow Jones account for 51 percent of the movement of that index.

In November 1999, the DJIA changed four members, adding Microsoft, Intel, SBC Communications, and Home Depot, while removing Sears, Union Carbide, Chevron, and Goodyear Tire. At this writing, the current divisor of the DJIA is .1768. Therefore, for

Dow Jones Industrial Average Stock Weightings

As of April 2000

STOCK	SYMBOL	WEIGHTING (AS OF 4/2000)
Intel	INTC	7.135%
Hewlett-Packard	HWP	6.535
JP Morgan	JPM	6.245
International Business Machines	IBM	5.456
Johnson & Johnson	JNJ	5.436
Minnesota Mining and Manufacturing	MMM	4.761
Microsoft	MSFT	4.269
Exxon Mobil	XOM	4.168
Merck & Co.	MRK	4.144
Citigroup	C	3.426
General Motors	GM	3.284
Eastman Kodak	EK	3.264
Coca-Cola	KO	3.170
United Technologies	UTX	3.166
Wal-Mart	WMT	3.065
Procter & Gamble	PG	2.988
American Express	AXP	2.782
General Electric	GE	2.718
Home Depot	HD	2.715
SBC Communications	SBC	2.458
DuPont	DD	2.421
Boeing	BA	2.320

SOURCE: BLOOMBERG L.P.

each one-point-up move in a stock, the DJIA moves up 5.66 points. If every stock in the Dow Jones were up or down one point, the Dow Jones would be up or down 169.68 points (**DOW JONES INDUSTRIAL AVERAGE STOCK WEIGHTINGS**). ❏

Using SPDRs and Other Products
to Diversify

There are many different products that help the investor
get diversification easily and quickly when the market and
sector indicators so dictate. Such products include the SPDRs
(SPY), Nasdaq 100 shares (QQQ), and many Select Sector
SPDRs, Merrill Lynch Sector Holders, and iShares.

OVER THE PAST FEW YEARS, the different exchanges have
devised new products that allow investors to gain diversification with
the purchase of one security. As long as you understand the weighting implications of such products, these can be very efficient ways to
play the broader market, or pinpoint a specific sector. For example,
instead of having to buy all 500 stocks in the S&P 500 (and weighting them accordingly), you can, in essence, own the S&P 500 with
one purchase using the S&P 500 Depositary Receipts, better known
as the SPDRs (SPY). There is a similar product available to trade in
the OTC market, that being the Nasdaq 100 Shares (QQQ).

These same types of products exist for the sectors. This is a newer
area of development for the exchanges, with some sectors still not
covered. But each day more sector products are introduced.

There are a couple of choices for sector (diversification) securities. The AMEX has Select SPDRs (nine in all), which are similar to
its SPYs, but are designed to cover a broad industry group, such as
financials (XLF), or technology (XLK). Merrill Lynch has come
out with what it calls HOLDRs, an example being its Biotech
HOLDRs (BBH). These HOLDRs cover more specific sectors or
subsectors. Also, Barclays has introduced iShares. Both Barclays
and Merrill Lynch have stated that they will continue to introduce
new exchange-traded funds in the future in an effort to cover more
and more sectors.

Regardless, whether it is the QQQ or the BBH, these investment
vehicles allow you to gain market or sector diversification with a

single transaction that otherwise would be difficult to achieve through outright ownership of all the underlying stocks. You are able to buy or sell them just like you would a stock, and since it is one easy transaction, it is a low-cost way to get diversified in the market or specific sector.

With the advent of these products, it becomes very easy to enter or exit the market or specific sector when the market (sector) indicators dictate. Using the bullish percent concept and sector relative strength tools, you can determine when to reenter the market or rotate to a given sector. So, for example, if the NYSE Bullish Percent reverses up from low levels, giving a buy signal, you can easily enter the market and gain instant diversification by buying the SPYs. Or let's say the drug sector bullish percent reverses up from low levels to give a buy signal and the relative strength for the group looks equally good. You can buy the Merrill Lynch Pharmaceutical HOLDRs (PPH) to gain instant diversification with one easy purchase. One note with respect to the HOLDRs is that they must be bought in lots of 100 shares.

Given how quickly the markets tend to move now, being able to get into the market or a given sector easily is of paramount importance. The vehicles discussed in this section provide that flexibility and can give you immediate diversification at the same time. ❏

P L A Y # 2 2

Market vs. Sector Timing

In the supermarket, each vegetable has its season.
Here in Virginia, we get strawberries in May, and we get
the best Hanover tomatoes in July. I don't try to make a
tomato sandwich in December. The result just isn't the same.
In the marketplace, we have the same phenomenon.
Every sector has its season, and knowing which sector is
in season can help your performance greatly.

CDA WIESENBERGER DID A fantastic study on sector rotation versus buy and hold versus market timing. Three hypothetical investors—Susan Selector, Timothy Timer, and Guy Buynhold—

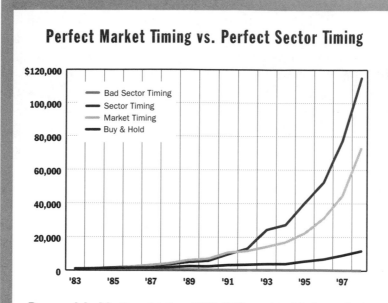

Perfect Market Timing vs. Perfect Sector Timing

Legend:
- Bad Sector Timing
- Sector Timing
- Market Timing
- Buy & Hold

Buy and hold. Bought the S&P 500 and held through the good times and bad times.

Market timing. Took money out of the S&P 500 before there was a down month and put it back in just before a positive month.

Sector timing. Bought the best-performing sector at the beginning of the year.

SOURCE: WWW.WIESENBERGER.COM. UNDERLYING DATA IS PROVIDED UPON REQUEST.

were created. Susan Selector chose the sector that is supposed to be the big hit the following year, and invests all of her money in that one sector. Timothy Timer is able to pull his money from the S&P 500, right before it has a down month, but is so smart he gets back in just before each positive gain month. Finally, there is Guy Buyn-hold. He doesn't believe in selling positions and just holds on for the long term. He puts his money in an S&P 500 Index and holds through thick and thin.

Each of the investors in the study began with $1,000 in 1983. For fifteen years they continue with their strategies, and at the end of 1998, let's see where they stand. Guy BuynHold ends up with $11,817 after fifteen years on an investment of $1,000. Not bad for no effort. Next, we have Timothy Timer. He turned his $1,000 into $73,000! A great return, but he had a lot of trading. Finally, there is Susan Selector. By just picking the biggest gaining sector of the year for fifteen straight years, she amassed over $115,000!

Of course no one is going to time the market perfectly like Timothy Timer, nor is anyone going to correctly pick the biggest gaining sector for the year fifteen years in a row. But what this study shows is the importance of sector timing in your portfolio picks. Sectors are like their own mini-markets, and understanding their individual bull and bear markets can make for much more fruitful investing (**PERFECT MARKET TIMING VS. PERFECT SECTOR TIMING**). ❑

PLAY #23

Which Side Are You On?:
Sector Bullish Percent Charts

*Buying low and selling high is the least risky
way to make money in the market.*

IT SEEMS THAT MANY investors are subscribing to the new paradigm of buying high and selling to a greater fool at a higher price. This may work, but it certainly is a risky proposition. Buying low and selling higher is a much less risky way to make money in a stock. The problem becomes determining what exactly is low. For this, we turn to our sector bullish percent work and present it in a unique format.

Everyone recalls the bell curve concept from the Statistics 101 class in college. When something you are evaluating is on the left-hand side of the curve, it is considered oversold in our Wall Street speak. We consider the right-hand side of the curve to be overbought, and the middle of the curve is normal. We have applied the bell curve concept to the sector bullish percent indicators we follow. Essentially, we have taken the vertical axis, which goes from 0 percent to 100 percent, and made it the horizontal axis. Then, the first four letters of each sector bullish percent are plotted on the curve. This gives us a composite picture of the risk in the market.

Sometimes, as in July 1999, the curve will get very skewed to the right-hand side, indicating an overbought market. Sometimes, as in October 1999, it will get very skewed to the left-hand side, indicating an oversold market. If you limit yourself to buying in sectors that are bullish and around 50 percent or lower, it forces you to buy when the risk is low and to be more defensive when the risk is high.

The beginning of 2000 presents another interesting situation. The Sector Bell Curve coming into the year 2000 really shows how the year 2000 played out. The bell curve was equally divided. Notice there were no sectors at the 50 percent line; everything was

SECTOR BULLISH PERCENT BELL CURVE LEGEND

AERO=Aerospace & Airlines	LEIS=Leisure
ASIA=Asia	MACH=Machinery & Tools
AUTO=Autos & Auto Parts	MEDI=Media
BANK=Banks	METL=Non-ferrous Metals
BIOM=Biotech	OIL=Oil
BUIL=Buildings	OILS=Oil Service
BUSI=Business Products &	PREC=Precious Metals
Services	PROT=Protection & Safety
CHEM=Chemicals	REAL=Real Estate
COMP=Computers	REST=Restaurant
DRUG=Drugs	RETL=Retail
ELEC=Electronics	SAVG=Savings & Loan
EURO=Europe	SEMI=Semiconductors
FINA=Finance	SOFT=Software
FOOD=Food, Beverage & Soap	STEE=Steel & Iron
FRST=Forest & Paper Products	TELE=Telephone
GAME=Gaming	TEXT=Textiles & Apparel
HEAL=Healthcare	TRAN=Non-air Transport
HOUS=Household Goods	EUTI=Electric Utilities
INSU=Insurance	GUTI=Gas Utilities
INET=Internet	WALL=Wall Street
LATI=Latin America	WAST=Waste Management

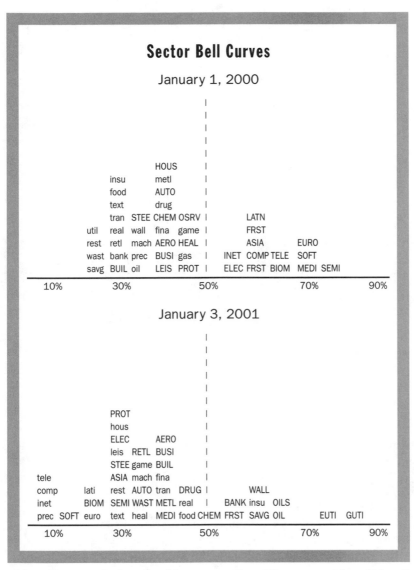

Sector Bell Curves

January 1, 2000

```
                                   |
                                   |
                                   |
                                   |
                     HOUS          |
          insu       metl          |
          food       AUTO          |
          text       drug          |
          tran STEE CHEM OSRV |         LATN
     util real wall fina game  |         FRST
     rest retl mach AERO HEAL  |         ASIA           EURO
     wast bank prec BUSI gas   |  INET COMP TELE  SOFT
     savg BUIL oil  LEIS PROT  |  ELEC FRST BIOM  MEDI SEMI
```

10%	30%	50%	70%	90%

January 3, 2001

```
                                   |
                                   |
                                   |
                                   |
                                   |
                                   |
          PROT                     |
          hous                     |
          ELEC      AERO           |
          leis RETL BUSI           |
          STEE game BUIL           |
     tele      ASIA mach fina      |
     comp lati rest AUTO tran DRUG |      WALL
     inet BIOM SEMI WAST METL real |  BANK insu  OILS
     prec SOFT euro text heal MEDI food CHEM FRST SAVG OIL    EUTI  GUTI
```

10%	30%	50%	70%	90%

either above or below the 50 percent line. The sectors that did well in 2000 were the sectors that were below the line, such as food, utilities, banks, savings and loan, restaurants, insurance, and others. The sectors that were above the 50 percent line suffered in 2000. Those sectors were the likes of semiconductors, media, Internet, telecommunications, and software. Coming into the year 2001, there are only a couple of sectors that are on the extremely over-

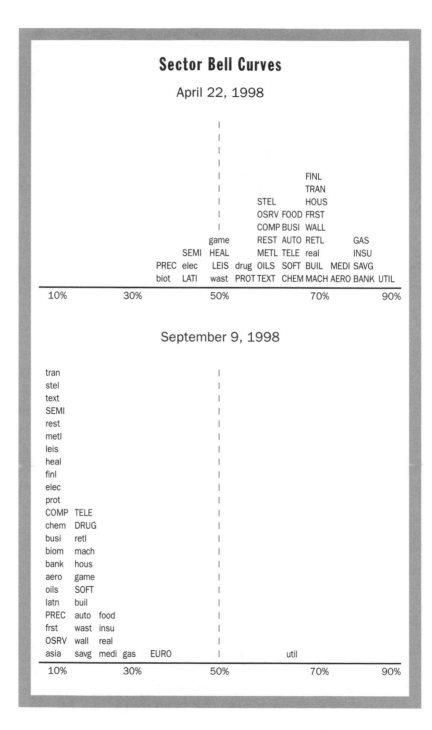

Sector Bell Curves

April 22, 1998

```
                                                        FINL
                                                        TRAN
                                             STEL        HOUS
                                             OSRV FOOD  FRST
                                             COMP BUSI  WALL
                              game           REST AUTO  RETL        GAS
                    SEMI     HEAL            METL TELE  real        INSU
           PREC     elec     LEIS  drug OILS SOFT BUIL  MEDI SAVG
           biot     LATI     wast  PROT TEXT CHEM MACH  AERO BANK UTIL
```
10%	30%	50%	70%	90%

September 9, 1998

```
tran                        |
stel                        |
text                        |
SEMI                        |
rest                        |
metl                        |
leis                        |
heal                        |
finl                        |
elec                        |
prot                        |
COMP  TELE                  |
chem  DRUG                  |
busi  retl                  |
biom  mach                  |
bank  hous                  |
aero  game                  |
oils  SOFT                  |
latn  buil                  |
PREC  auto  food            |
frst  wast  insu            |
OSRV  wall  real            |
asia  savg  medi  gas  EURO |              util
```
10%	30%	50%	70%	90%

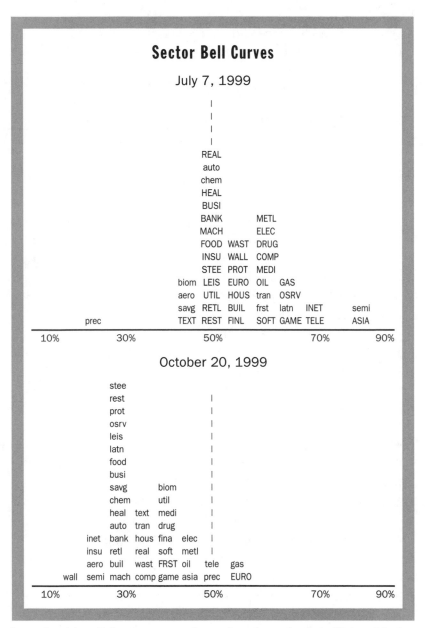

Sector Bell Curves

July 7, 1999

```
                            |
                            |
                            |
                            |
                          REAL
                          auto
                          chem
                          HEAL
                          BUSI
                          BANK        METL
                          MACH        ELEC
                          FOOD WAST   DRUG
                          INSU WALL   COMP
                          STEE PROT   MEDI
                     biom LEIS EURO   OIL  GAS
                     aero UTIL HOUS   tran OSRV
                     savg RETL BUIL   frst latn  INET        semi
          prec       TEXT REST FINL   SOFT GAME  TELE        ASIA
   10%          30%            50%              70%          90%
```

October 20, 1999

```
          stee
          rest                    |
          prot                    |
          osrv                    |
          leis                    |
          latn                    |
          food                    |
          busi                    |
          savg      biom          |
          chem      util          |
          heal text medi          |
          auto tran drug          |
     inet bank hous fina elec     |
     insu retl real soft metl     |
     aero buil wast FRST oil  tele gas
wall semi mach comp game asia prec EURO
   10%          30%            50%              70%          90%
```

bought side of the curve, such as electric and gas utilities. Notice how those sectors that started out 2000 on the right-hand side of the curve are now on the left-hand side, and vice versa. In fact, starting in 2001, 79 percent of the sectors are at the 50 percent mark or lower. Review some of the "compare and contrast" curves from markets past and we think you'll have to agree—a picture speaks a thousand words (**BELL CURVE CHARTS,** pages 65–67). ❏

It Feels Like the Bullish Percent Should Be at 10 Percent!

THE PAIN IMPOSED from technology stocks' performance during 2000 was unprecedented for many investors. The Nasdaq Composite was down more than 50 percent from its March 2000 highs. Stocks like Redhat (RHAT) had fallen over 90 percent that year. That's right, over 90 percent! In fact, during 2000 16.5 percent of the stocks on the Nasdaq were down 20 percent or more. With returns like that, one might expect that the NYSE or at least the OTC Bullish Percent would be down at 2 percent! There are in fact many times when one might expect the bullish percent to be extremely low, but it is not. Why might that be? The answer, simply, is sector rotation. The markets of 1994 and 2000 had a lot of similarities. Let's look at some aspects of those markets that will likely happen again.

ONE STOCK, ONE VOTE

IF YOU RECALL, a bullish percent is calculated by dividing the number of stocks on a point and figure buy signal by the total number of stocks in the universe. Essentially there are two piles of stocks: a buy signal pile and a sell signal pile. Once the stock is in the sell signal pile, it remains there until a buy signal is given. The stock can continue to give multiple sell signals, but once its vote has been counted, then multiple sell signals don't count. This is different from a price-weighted or capitalization-weighted index. In a price-weighted index, the higher the price, the more votes the stock gets. In a capitalization-weighted index, the bigger the stocks' market capitalization, the more votes it receives.

The same goes with numerous other stocks. For instance, in 2000, Copper Mountain Networks (CMTN) moved from a buy signal to a sell signal at $42. This is when the sell signal vote for CMTN counted in the OTC Bullish Percent. Since that sell signal, the stock has given several more and fallen to $6.25. During that drop, CMTN gave six different sell signals, although only that first sell signal at 42 counted in the calculation of the bullish percent.

If the weak get weaker and the strong get stronger, the Bullish Percent reading can remain the same. That is the design of the indicator. It is created to measure supply and demand changes in the marketplace. In the case of CMTN there has been no change in the supply and demand picture. Supply has remained in control.

SECTOR ROTATION

THOSE OF YOU in this business in 1994 will remember that the year was marked by a lot of sector rotation while the broad indices held up and came in basically flat for the year. In 1994, you came into the office and waited for the next sector to get hit and taken out to the woodshed. In fact, 80 percent of the stocks were down 20 percent or more at some time during the year. It's just that those 80 percent of stocks weren't all down 20 percent at the same time. Sector by sector, they all rotated into oversold territory at 30 percent or below on their sector bullish percent charts (or at least close to that 30 percent level). Had every sector seen its low at the same time, like 1987, 1990, or 1998, then you would have gotten an NYSE Bullish Percent reading of 20 percent or lower instead of the low being 32.1 percent in December.

Look at the breakdown of when sector bullish percents made their lows in 1994. You can see that it is spread across the year, but the month with the most bottoms is December. Now take a look at the 2000 Sector Bullish Percent Lows. You will find a very similar picture. Some sectors hit a low early in the year, while others are just making their low sector reading.

1994 SECTOR BULLISH PERCENT LOWS
◆ **February**
   Metals non-ferrous at 30 percent

◆ **April**

Drug at 18 percent

Gaming at 10 percent

Precious metals at 26 percent

Protection and safety equipment at 32 percent

Telephone at 30 percent

◆ **May**

Electronics at 42 percent

Finance at 26 percent

Food, beverage, and soap at 36 percent

Forest and paper products at 42 percent

Media at 36 percent

Steel and iron at 26 percent

◆ **June**

Computer at 30 percent

◆ **July**

Health care at 34 percent

◆ **September**

Electric utilities at 24 percent

◆ **December**

Aerospace/airlines at 32 percent

Autos and auto parts at 30 percent

Banks at 42 percent

Buildings at 28 percent

Business products at 36 percent

Chemicals at 40 percent

Household goods at 38 percent

Leisure at 34 percent

Machinery and tools at 36 percent

Real estate at 26 percent

Restaurants at 30 percent

Retailing at 30 percent

Savings and loan at 42 percent

Gas utilities at 14 percent

Wall Street at 22 percent

Waste management at 30 percent

◆ **January 1995**
   Oil at 32 percent
◆ **February 1995**
   Oil service at 26 percent

2000 SECTOR BULLISH PERCENT LOWS
◆ **January**
   Food, beverage, and soap (December 1999) at 30 percent
   Savings and loan at 16 percent
   Textile and apparel (December 1999) at 30 percent
   Waste management (December 1999) at 24 percent
◆ **February**
   Gas utilities at 38 percent
◆ **March**
   Banks at 10 percent
   Buildings at 28 percent
   Insurance at 20 percent
   Real estate at 28 percent
   Transports non-air at 26 percent
   Electric utilities at 26 percent
◆ **April**
   Biomedics/genetics at 8 percent
   Computers at 14 percent
   Drugs at 26 percent
   Electronics at 28 percent
   Health care at 28 percent
   Internet at 4 percent
   Media at 20 percent
   Semiconductors at 6 percent
   Software at 10 percent
   Telephone at 12 percent
   Wall Street at 28 percent
◆ **May**
   Retail at 30 percent
   Steel and iron at 20 percent

◆ **June**

Restaurants at 34 percent

◆ **September**

Auto and auto parts at 26 percent

Europe at 12 percent

◆ **October**

Aerospace/airlines at 22 percent

Asia/Pacific at 22 percent

Business products and services at 28 percent

Chemicals at 28 percent

Finance at 30 percent

Forest and paper products at 12 percent

Machinery and tools at 26 percent

Metals non-ferrous at 24 percent

◆ **November**

Gaming at 40 percent

Household goods at 34 percent

Latin America at 28 percent

Leisure at 34 percent

Oil at 52 percent

Oil service at 32 percent

Precious metals at 10 percent

Protection and safety equipment at 26 percent

PLAY #25

Sector Relative Strength

Sector relative strength is a great tool to use when trying to determine which sectors are outperforming the market. Given the fact that the sector is the greatest contributor to price fluctuation in a stock, it is extremely important to determine the relative strength. Focus on sectors exhibiting positive relative strength (those in a column of Xs on their RS chart).

RELATIVE STRENGTH IS AN important term, which we use extensively and on which we place great importance. Many of you are very aware of its definition and importance pertaining to stock

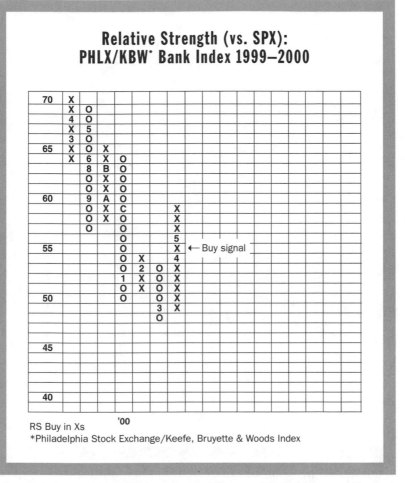

**Relative Strength (vs. SPX):
PHLX/KBW* Bank Index 1999–2000**

RS Buy in Xs   '00
*Philadelphia Stock Exchange/Keefe, Bruyette & Woods Index

selection, but sector relative strength is considered an equally vital component of technical analysis. During times of market uncertainty, Sector RS takes on a particularly significant role. It is at these times that you should be paying close attention to sectors that are exhibiting strong relative strength—those that are showing that they are "outperforming" the market.

Sector relative strength measures how a particular sector is doing compared to the market in general. The relative strength calculation is simply done (using Tuesday evening closing data) by dividing the price of the sector by the price of the S&P 500 (SPX), and then multiplying by 100. This number can then be

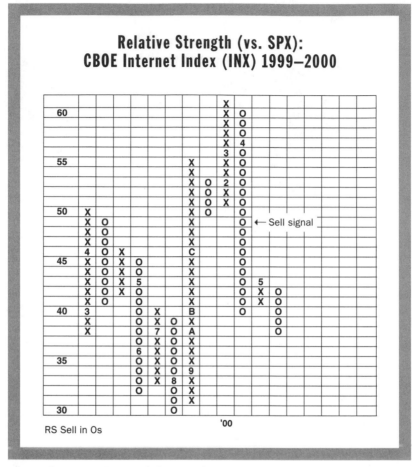

Relative Strength (vs. SPX): CBOE Internet Index (INX) 1999–2000

RS Sell in Os

plotted on a point and figure chart. Relative strength buy signals are given when a column of Xs exceeds a previous column of Xs. Sell signals are given when a column of Os exceeds a previous column of Os. But of equal importance for Sector RS is what the most recent column is on the RS chart. When a sector index reverses up into a column of Xs on its RS chart, we consider that a buy signal. When such a reversal up occurs, you can buy index calls on the specific index or can look to buy the best-looking large-cap stock in the particular index. As an example, if the Semiconductor Index (SOX) reversed up into a column of Xs on its RS chart, you could buy index calls several months out (at-the-money) or you could buy Intel (INTC). When a sector index reverses down into a column of Os on its RS chart, we consider it a warning sign or sell signal—it suggests that that sector is likely to underperform the market in general. So when trying to determine which sectors to focus on, stick with those that have just reversed up into Xs or are continuing to put in more Xs on their RS charts (**RELATIVE STRENGTH (VS. SPX): PHLX/KBW BANK INDEX 1999–2000**, page 73, and **RELATIVE STRENGTH (VS. SPX): CBOE INTERNET INDEX (INX) 1999–2000**, left). ❑

Summary:
Index/SPX x 100=Sector RS Reading
Sector RS in a Column of Xs=Outperformance
Sector RS in a Column of Os=Underperformance

▰▰▰ P L A Y # 2 6 ▰▰▰

It's an Art, Not a Science

Many times a sector will create its own "red"
and "green" zones. Be alert for those zones,
because they will present opportunities.

IF YOU HAVE READ *Point and Figure Charting* (Wiley, 1995) by Tom Dorsey, you are familiar with the sector bullish percent concept. It never hurts to periodically review such an important concept. A sector bullish percent measures the percentage of stocks within a particular industry group that are on a point and figure buy signal. This percentage is plotted on a grid from 0 percent to 100 percent. In short, when the sector bullish percent chart is in a column of Xs it means the offensive team is on the field with respect to that sector, and a column of Os means the defensive team is on the field.

Also very important to the interpretation of that sector bullish percent is the field position. The 70 percent level and above is considered to be the "red" zone or high-risk area. The 30 percent level and below is considered the "green" zone or low-risk area. Once a sector gets to the 70 percent level, all of the people who want to be invested in that group are probably already in, and thus the availability of demand to continue to push the sector

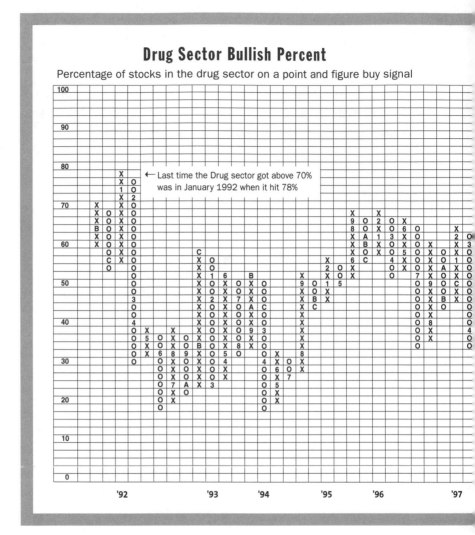

Drug Sector Bullish Percent
Percentage of stocks in the drug sector on a point and figure buy signal

← Last time the Drug sector got above 70% was in January 1992 when it hit 78%

higher is extremely limited. Conversely, when a sector gets to 30 percent or lower, it means that almost everyone who wants to sell has already done so. Thus, the availability of supply to continue to push the sector lower is extremely limited.

The 30 percent and 70 percent levels are not set in stone. For instance, we follow over forty different sector bullish percents. Each one takes on its own personality, so to speak, just like children or grandchildren do. Look at the chart of the drug sector bullish percent. Barring some very washed-out market conditions, like 1987,

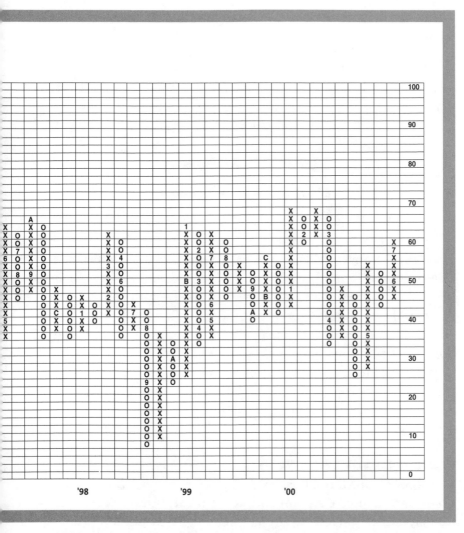

1990, and 1998, the drug sector tends to bottom out in the 34 percent to 40 percent area. Therefore, if you waited to buy the drug stocks until after they had fallen to the 30 percent level or lower and then reversed up, you would have missed a lot of great moves in the sector. The same is also true of the drug sector at the top. This sector tends to top out in the upper 60 percent level. In fact, it hasn't been above 70 percent since January 1992, when the sector got as high as 78 percent.

For some sectors, the tops and bottoms seem to come at the 30 percent and 70 percent level like clockwork. The red and green zones for other sectors, such as drugs, media, and chemicals, seem to come just above the 30 percent level and just below the 70 percent level. In yet other sectors, getting down to 20 percent or 10 percent is not that uncommon, nor is getting to the 80 percent or 90 percent level. Two examples of the latter would be semiconductors and precious metals. (**DRUG BULLISH PERCENT**, pages 76–77). ❑

PLAY # 2 7

Market Leadership

Being the most popular in class does pay off.

IN ANY MARKET, there are some sectors that do better than others. In bullish markets, there are always segments of the market that carry the indices to new highs. In neutral markets, one or two industries always continue to forge ahead, while most others mark time. In bearish markets, there are some sectors that don't decline as much. How do you identify market leadership? We use four indicators for each sector, which give us a composite picture of how that sector is stacking up compared to others. There are over forty sectors that we measure with the following four criteria:

SECTOR RELATIVE STRENGTH

WE USE AN EQUAL DOLLAR weighting index of stocks created in-house and then take a point and figure relative strength reading for that index. The relative strength reading is calculated by dividing the price of the index by the S&P 500 and then multiplying by 100. Once that reading is obtained, it is plotted on a point and figure chart. Every index has a price chart and a relative strength chart. The strongest are those whose relative strength charts are in a column of Xs, as that tells us the sector is outperforming the market as a whole. You can also look at the relative strength chart of the sector indices that trade options on the Philadelphia Stock Exchange, American Stock Exchange, Chicago Board Options Exchange, or Pacific Stock Exchange.

PERCENT OF STOCKS ON A RELATIVE STRENGTH BUY SIGNAL

THE POINT AND FIGURE RELATIVE strength buy and sell signals are long-term in nature, lasting an average of two years. Within an industry group, we calculate the percentage of stocks whose relative strength charts are on buy signals. This percentage is then plotted on a grid from 0 percent to 100 percent. When it is in a column of Xs and rising, it means more stocks underlying that sector are getting stronger versus the market on a long-term basis.

PERCENT OF STOCKS IN A COLUMN OF Xs ON THEIR RS CHARTS

WITHIN EACH INDUSTRY GROUP, we calculate the number of stocks whose individual relative strength charts are outperforming the market on a short-term basis. Though signals on average last two years or more, a change in columns on the relative strength chart lasts generally six to eight months. This percentage is also plotted on a grid from 0 percent to 100 percent, and when this indicator is in Xs and moving higher, it suggests the sector is performing better than the market on a short-term basis.

PERCENT OF STOCKS WITH A POSITIVE TREND

WHEN A STOCK IS TRADING above the bullish support line, we say its main trend is positive. The basic tenet here is the more stocks that are in positive trends, the stronger the sector. The percent of stocks with positive trends is plotted on a grid from 0 percent to 100 percent. Like the other indicators, we want this to be in a column of Xs and rising.

Looking at these four sector indicators together gives us a composite picture of just how strong that sector is compared to the overall market. When initiating new positions, focus on those sectors where at least three of these indicators are positive. This is true whether you are a short-term trader or a long-term investor. In market declines, you're likely not to lose as much ground, and in market advances these sectors will lead the way. Even for short-term investors, you want to be in the sectors that are moving the market, because this is where most of the action lies. ❏

Dow Jones 20 Bond Average

Having a reliable bond indicator is important not only with respect to your fixed-income investments, but also in guiding you with investments in financially related sectors. The Dow Jones 20 Bond Average is our bond indicator of choice.

THE DOW JONES 20 Bond Average (DJBB) is our primary interest rate indicator and has been one of the best indicators we have seen. This obscure index is comprised of ten long-term industrial bonds and ten long-term utility bonds. We plot this index on a point and figure chart using a .20 box size. Like all point and figure charts we keep, it requires a three-box move to cause a reversal, which would be .60 in this case. The chart is then maintained like any other.

When reading the DJBB chart, we are looking for two types of buy signals. The first is a *double top break*. This is the simplest of buy signals and occurs when a column of Xs exceeds the previous column of Xs. The second signal is called a *low pole warning*. In this case, the chart exceeds the previous bottom by at least three Os and then reverses back to the upside and retraces the previous down move by greater than 50 percent.

The opposite is true when looking at sell signals. When a *double bottom break*, the simplest of sell signals, is given, the chart is on a sell signal. A *high pole warning* is also considered a signal to move to the sidelines. Opposite of the low pole warning, this occurs when the chart exceeds a previous top by three or more boxes and then pulls back by greater than 50 percent of the previous up move.

The chart on pages 82–83 has given many timely signals. These signals are outlined below. Following this one bond indicator, imagine the money you could have made in bonds or bond funds, or just knowing when to lock in your mortgage (**DOW JONES 20 BOND AVERAGE 1992–2000**).

◆ **May 1992.** The chart broke a double top at 99.20. It stayed on a buy signal, indicating lower rates, until November 1993. The chart gave subsequent buy signals at 102.60 in January 1993 and 104.60 in April 1993. The chart was on a buy signal for approximately one-and-one-half years.

◆ **November 1993.** The chart broke a double bottom at 105.60. It had been on a buy signal since May 1992. This sell signal led to higher interest rates and three more sell signals. The chart eventually bottomed at 93.60 before the chart managed to move back to a buy signal. We advised all of our clients to lock in their adjustable rate mortgages.

◆ **January 1995.** This double top break at 94.60 lasted about seven months and led to a move to 103.60 before it gave a sell signal.

◆ **July 1995.** This was a short-lived sell signal. The chart broke a double bottom at 102.80 and fell to 102 before it was able to reverse back to the upside and give a low pole warning.

◆ **September 1995.** The DJBB managed to retrace greater than 50 percent of the previous decline, giving a low pole warning at 103. This put the chart back on a buy signal. The buy signal led to a breakout at 103.80 and eventually a high on the chart at 106 in February 1996.

◆ **March 1996.** After reaching 106, the chart pulled back, giving a high pole warning at 103.80. This signal indicated higher interest rates and led to two sell signals on the chart, which fell to 101 in July 1996.

◆ **August 1996.** The chart exceeded a previous top, moving the index back on a buy signal, suggesting lower rates. The break was followed by another buy signal and a high of 104 in November 1996.

◆ **January 1997.** A double bottom was broken at 103, moving the DJBB back to a sell signal. In April, the chart had fallen to 101.20.

◆ **June 1997.** The chart rallied in June to give a low pole warning indicating higher prices from this index and lower rates. The chart then gave three double top buy signals, reaching a new chart high of 107 in October 1998.

◆ **February 1999.** A double bottom was given, moving the chart to a sell signal. This sell signal led to six more double bottom breaks by February 2000 and a low of 95.

◆ **February 2000.** The chart gave a short-lived low pole warning, the first such warning on the chart that did not lead to a buy sig-

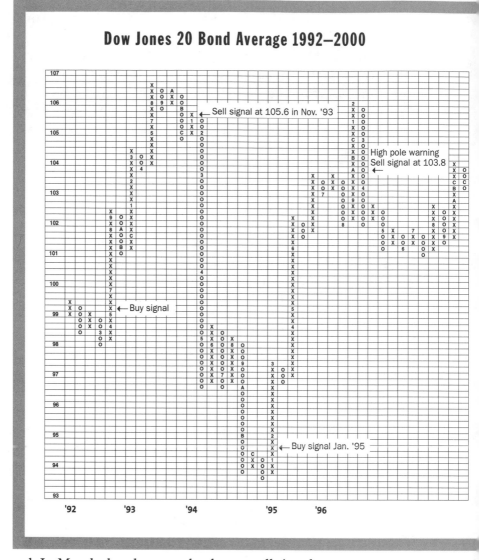

Dow Jones 20 Bond Average 1992–2000

nal. In March the chart was back on a sell signal.

◆ **March 2000.** The index failed to get through resistance at 96.40 and broke a double bottom, moving back to a sell signal and thus indicating higher rates.

◆ **June 2000.** The Dow Jones 20 Bond Average fell from the March sell signal at 95.6 down to a low of 93.4 before giving a low pole warning at 94.6. Note that the Dow Jones 20 Bond Average

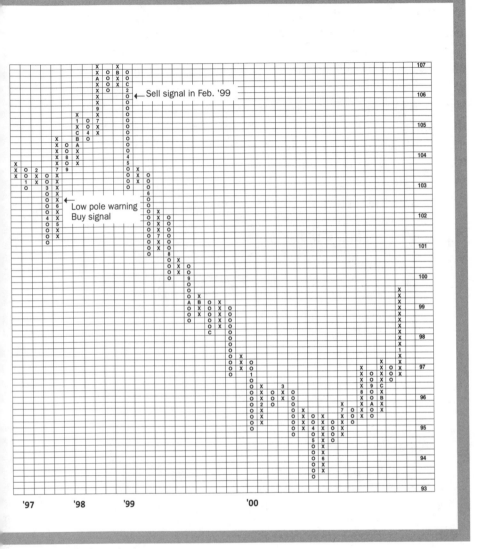

has now fallen slightly further than its December 1994 lows of 93.6.

◆ **September 2000.** A high pole warning was given at 96 to move one back to the sidelines on bonds after a profitable upside trade from June to September. Notice, though, that the Dow Jones 20 Bond Average continues to make overall higher bottoms after bottoming out at 93.4, right at the same area it bottomed in December 1994.

◆ **December 2000.** The low pole warning in September did not result in an actual sell signal and the series of higher bottoms was maintained. The Dow Jones 20 Bond Average goes back to a buy signal with the double top breakout at 97.2. At this writing, this bond average has rallied to 99.6 and remains on a buy signal.

THERE HAVE BEEN FOURTEEN SIGNALS in the Dow Jones 20 Bond Average since 1992, and eleven of those signals have resulted in profitable trades. That is being right almost 80 percent of the time—not a bad percentage, and these signals kept you out of bonds in the disastrous 1994 and 1999 markets and in them for the nice rally in 1995. The point is that not every signal, whether buy or sell, will be right, but you want to play each one accordingly, given the track record of this indicator.

CHAPTER

4

ESSENTIALS OF STOCK SELECTION

TRAINING CAMP IS OVER and the season is starting. Come Sunday afternoon, the team must be ready, as a unit, to go out on the field. But no team can be successful without each individual football player being equally prepared and motivated. This combination increases the probability of victory for the team. In the past chapters, we have provided you with rules of the game and other macro components that make up the playbook. Market psychology gets you in the right mindset to play, while market and sector applications determine what stadium you are playing in and which team is on the field, offense or defense. This chapter will deal with the essentials of individual stock selection to ensure you are putting the right player on the field.

PLAY #29

Four Steps for Initiating New Positions

WE RECOMMEND A top-down approach to investing. In light of that, we designed a four-step process that you should go through when initiating new positions.

STEP 1: Market. What to do: Use the NYSE Bullish Percent, Option Stock Bullish Percent, OTC Bullish Percent, High-Low Index, Ten Week, and other indicators to determine if you play offense or defense.

STEP 2: Sector. What to do: Determine which sectors suggest offense (and what their respective field position is)—those in a column of Xs on their sector bullish percent chart. It is best to stay with sectors that are bullish and below 50 percent. Determine how a sector is doing relative to the S&P 500. Ideally, you want to invest in sectors that are outperforming the SPX (those that are in a column of Xs on their RS chart).

STEP 3: Fundamentals. What to do: Create and maintain an inventory of stocks to work from. Use any number of sources available to determine which stocks are fundamentally sound. In this step you are pinpointing which specific stock to buy.

STEP 4: Technicals. What to do: Review fundamentally sound stocks on a technical basis to cull those controlled by demand, those that demonstrate the best technical picture. This will narrow your fundamental inventory down to those issues with the best probability of moving higher. In this step you are determining when to buy a specific stock.

In summary, try to follow this four-step checklist when initiating new positions. By paying attention to the market and the sector risks (opportunities), and then coupling the fundamentals with the technicals, your odds of success should increase. Not every trade will work out, but this gives you a definable game plan, something most investors don't have. Stick to the plan, make your decision, then manage the outcome. ❏

Stock Evaluation Checklist: Evaluating Technical Pros and Cons

STEP FOUR OF the preceding checklist involves evaluating the technical pros and cons of a stock. The checklist that we provide below can be helpful with this step.

We recommend that you literally go through and evaluate the technical merits of each stock you are considering buying. Once you have determined a fundamentally sound inventory to work from, go through and write down the pros and cons (technical picture) of each stock you are considering for purchase. The

Stock Evaluation Checklist—Pros and Cons

Stock: _____ Date: _____

	POSITIVE	NEGATIVE	COMMENTS
Market	___	___	_____
Sector	___	___	_____
Sector RS	___	___	_____
Trend	___	___	_____
RS	___	___	_____
Peer RS	___	___	_____
Pattern	___	___	_____
Price Objective	___	___	_____
Risk-Reward	___	___	_____
Momentum	___	___	_____
Trading Band	___	___	_____

Stock Evaluation Checklist

Stock: Stock A   **Date:** _____

	POSITIVE	NEGATIVE	COMMENTS
Market	X		OTC/Opti BP in Xs
Sector		X	In Xs but 64%
Sector RS	X		Index & DWA in Xs
Trend	X		Just held BSL
RS	X		RS Buy in Xs
Peer RS	X		RS Buy in Xs
Pattern	X		Big Base Breakout
Price Objective	X		Horizontal = 84
Risk-Reward	X		45 / 10 = 4.5 to 1
Momentum	X	X	Month+/Wkly -
Trading Band		X	Slightly overbought

Conclusion: This is an example of how a completed stock evaluation might look. In this evaluation example, you can see the weight of the evidence is in your favor.

checklist on the previous page can help you accomplish this. You can use this as a template to help you map out your stock decisions. Basically, it is the old saying, "A picture paints a thousand words." You will be able to clearly see in writing the positives and negatives of each stock. Hopefully this will help you make sound, clear-cut decisions, without emotion.

When trying to narrow down your list, you should ideally focus on stocks that are in an overall uptrend (trading above their bullish support line), have positive relative strength versus the market and their peers, are on a point and figure buy signal on their trend chart, have positive momentum, and present a good risk-reward ratio (**STOCK EVALUATION CHECKLIST—PROS AND CONS** and **STOCK EVALUATION CHECKLIST**, above). ❏

Bullish Support Line

The Bullish Support Line is one of the two main trendlines
used in the point and figure methodology. This trendline
is also called the uptrend line. Typically, it is best to buy
stocks that are trading above their bullish support line.

THE BULLISH SUPPORT LINE is drawn when the stock has
formed an apparent bottom. It should be started in the box directly below the lowest O in the lowest column on the trend chart, and
then should move upward to the right at a 45-degree angle. If the
stock is trading above this bullish support line, it is considered to be
in an overall uptrend. A stock will often pull back right to the bullish support line and will hold, only to resume its upward bias. In
essence, the trendline acts as a brick wall.

Trendlines can be very helpful when making buy and sell decisions. Ideally, investors want to buy or hold stocks that are in an
overall uptrend, moving higher. When the bullish support line is
broken or penetrated, it signals a change in the trend of the stock
to negative, and suggests it is time to evaluate whether the stock
should be sold (**BOEING COMPANY (BA): BULLISH SUPPORT LINE**, pages
92–93). ❏

Bearish Resistance Line

The bearish resistance line is one of the two main trendlines
used in the point and figure methodology. This trendline is
also called the "downtrend line." Typically, it is best to stay
away from stocks trading below their bearish resistance line.

THE BEARISH RESISTANCE LINE is drawn when the stock has
formed an apparent top. It should be started in the box directly
above the highest X in the highest column on the trend chart, and
then should move downward to the right at a 45-degree angle. If
the stock is trading below this bearish resistance line, it is consid-

Boeing Company (BA): Bullish Support Line

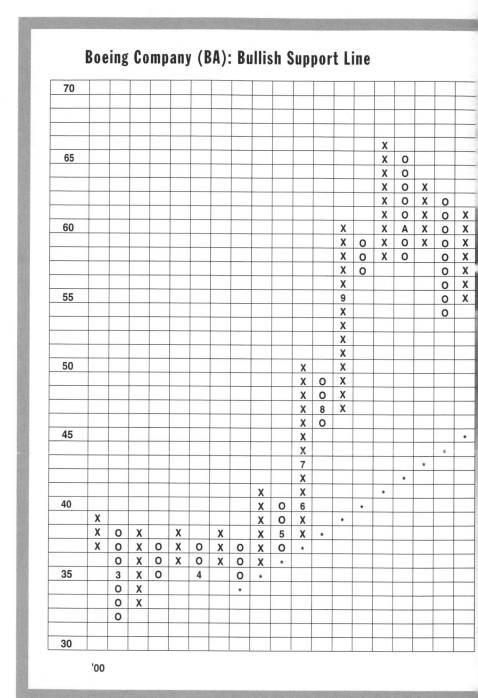

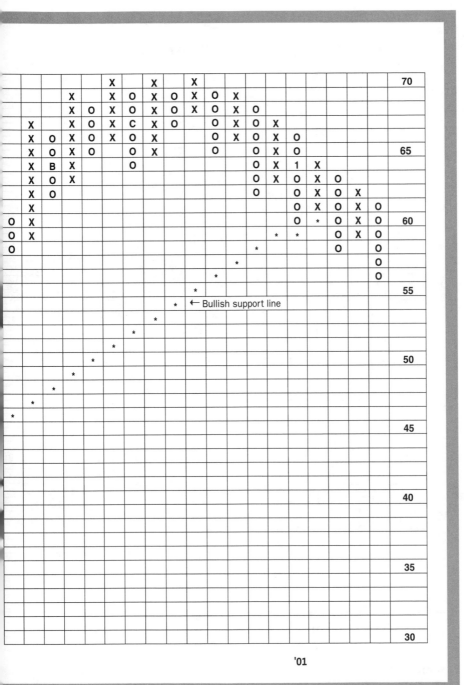

← Bullish support line

'01

Tupperware (TUP): Bearish Resistance Line

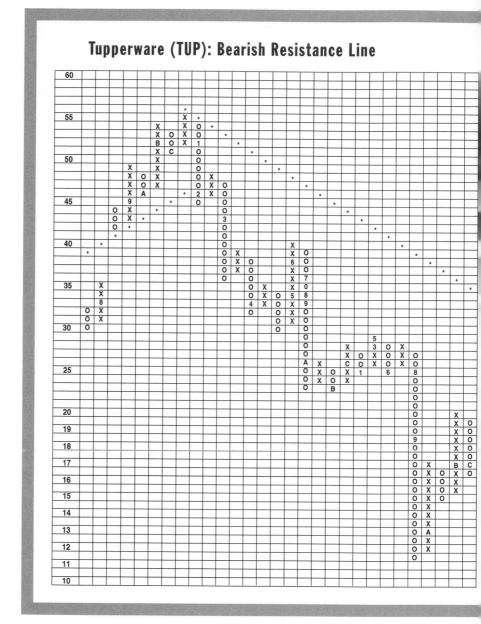

ered to be in an overall downtrend. A stock will often rally right back up to the bearish resistance line and will be repelled, only to resume its downward bias. Again, the trendline acts as a brick wall.

Trendlines can be very helpful when making buy and sell deci-

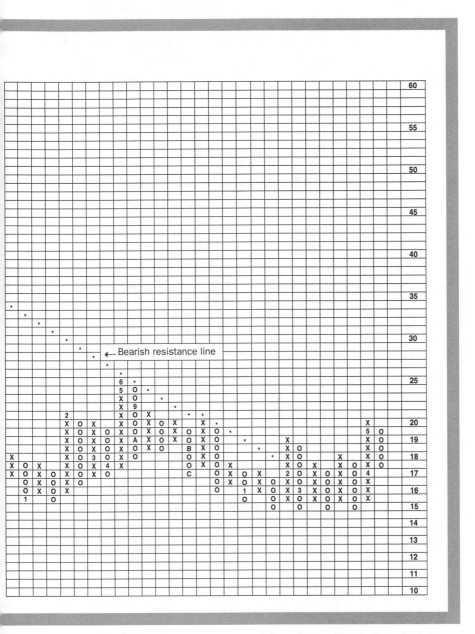

Bearish resistance line

sions. Ideally, investors want to avoid stocks trading below their bearish resistance line, since they are considered in an overall downtrend. When the bearish resistance line is broken or penetrated,
though, it signals a change in the trend of the stock to positive, and

suggests it is time to evaluate whether that stock should be bought. In such a case, it is often a sign that the stock has made a bottom and is a good turnaround candidate. Watch for stocks to change trend in this fashion, especially if the stock has been trading below its bearish resistance line for a long time, as these are candidates for purchase (**TUPPERWARE (TUP): BEARISH RESISTANCE LINE,** pages 94–95). ❑

Relative Strength: Motorboat vs. Rowboat

Think of a stock's relative strength as having a motor in your boat. It is much easier to move through choppy waters or go upstream when you have a motorboat versus a rowboat. A stock that exhibits positive relative strength has a "motor" in it; stick with stocks that have positive RS, as they will have an easier time navigating the uncertain waters of the stock market.

RELATIVE STRENGTH READINGS are incredibly important in stock selection in all kinds of markets. The relative strength calculation is done simply by dividing the price of the stock by the price of the Dow, or any index you choose, and then multiplying by 1,000. This number can then be plotted on a point and figure chart. RS chart buy signals are given when a column of Xs exceeds a previous column of Xs. Sell signals are given when a column of Os exceeds a previous column of Os. In the case of RS charts, the pattern is irrelevant. Relative strength signals generally last about two years and tell the overall trend of a stock. Positive relative strength suggests the stock will outperform the market, while negative relative strength suggests the stock will underperform the market. It's also important to watch for RS column reversals for short-term guidance. So the best combination for a stock's RS reading would be on an RS buy signal and in a column of Xs moving up. This would suggest that a stock is outperforming the market in both a short- and long-term respect. The worst RS combination is on an RS sell signal and in a column of Os.

Let's look at an example of RS:
◆ Say, for instance, that XYZ was at $85 and the Dow was at 11,500.

◆ If we divided $85 by 11,500 and moved the decimal, we would get 7.39.

◆ We would plot this number on the RS chart of XYZ.

◆ Let's say the following week the stock falls to $80 and the Dow dropped to 10,000. (We do our relative strength calculations once a week using Tuesday's closing data.)

◆ We now divide $80 by 10,000 and get eight.

◆ In this case the stock dropped and the Dow dropped, but the relative strength chart went up.

This tells us that the stock is doing better than the Dow—it is exhibiting positive RS, and it is possible that the only reason it is down is because the overall market has dragged it down. This stock is likely to be one of the first to snap back when the overall market does. So when investing, it is best to focus on stocks that have positive relative strength. Also, when trying to decide which stocks to keep and which to sell (when trying to move to a more defensive posture than the market indicators suggest), keep the stocks that are exhibiting positive RS and consider selling the stocks with negative relative strength.

In summary, relative strength is a form of measuring a stock's individual performance. Positive relative strength suggests the stock will outperform the broad market averages. Negative relative strength suggests the stock will underperform the broad market averages. As the name implies, relative strength is a measure of relative performance, not absolute performance. When buying stocks, focus on those that are a "motorboat" rather than a "rowboat"— those with positive RS. You will likely have an easier trip upstream (against the market) and will be less likely to capsize. ❏

PLAY #34

Good Stocks Stand Out in Market Declines

There is a silver lining in every dark cloud.

IT IS A FACT OF LIFE in the market that you will experience both bull and bear markets. The good news is that the bull markets last much longer than the bear markets. Investors who keep their eyes open can typically find good opportunities when the market falls. This is because we often see good stocks act well during declines in the market.

This is not to say that the stock has to rally while the overall market is falling. The stock could move sideways while the market or the sector to which it belongs heads south. It may even fall a little bit but not as much as the market. If you own the stock, you may not be happy that it is moving down, but if the market falls 15 percent and your stock drops by only 5 percent, that is good performance relative to the market.

Step back and think about it for a minute, though. The irrefutable law of supply and demand is what moves stocks. If you see a stock moving sideways during a market decline, it suggests there is enough demand for that stock to offset all of the supply. With most stocks falling during a decline, there is selling pressure on the vast majority of stocks.

Yet here is a stock that is bucking that trend. It is not moving up, but it's not moving down, either, and that is because of the demand for the stock. Once the selling pressure from the market decline is finished, demand usually remains strong. Not only that, but the investors who were buying the stock during the decline are not likely to sell soon, since they just purchased the stock and are expecting it to move higher. That means there is less supply of the stock to put on the market, and this, too, is good. The point is you can use market declines to try to find stocks that are holding up well.

Relative strength is a good tool to use to help you in this process. You will also want to note that stocks that hold up well are often market leaders once the market turns back up.

We should mention one caveat here, however. When the market does decline sharply, you will often see a flight to higher yielding stocks. The thinking is that the yield will offer the stock some support, since investors will pay for the dividend. So be careful that any list you keep of stocks holding up well in a falling market are not all high-yielding stocks. ❑

Best in Class: Using Peer Relative Strength to Buy the Best Stock in a Given Sector

Relative strength is a very important component of stock selection. Not only is it important to focus on stocks exhibiting positive relative strength versus the market, but it is equally important to focus on stocks exhibiting positive relative strength versus their peers—other stocks within the sector. Doing this allows you to invest in stocks considered "best in class," or those performing the best within a given sector.

RELATIVE STRENGTH (RS) is a form of measuring a stock's individual performance versus some other vehicle. In the case of peer RS, you are evaluating how a given stock is doing versus its sector (stocks that make up a given sector). For example, the peer RS reading would measure how Intel (INTC) is doing relative to other semiconductor stocks.

Peer RS becomes important when you are trying to narrow down the list of potential stocks to buy in a given sector. Like other relative strength charts, you want to focus on stocks whose peer RS chart is on a buy signal and in a column of Xs—that is the best combination for a relative strength reading, and the RS is therefore said to be "positive." If the stock has positive peer RS, it is outperforming other stocks in its sector. These are the stocks to focus on when buying within a given group.

The calculation for peer RS is very simple. It is done each Tuesday, based on the closing prices of that day. The closing price of the stock is divided by the closing price of the applicable index. In the same example, Intel's (INTC) Tuesday closing price would be divided by the closing price of the Dorsey, Wright Semiconductor Index (DWASEMI). The resulting number would then be plotted on a relative strength chart.

The RS is said to be on a buy signal (or positive) if the most recent signal on the RS chart is a buy signal (a column of Xs exceeding a previous column of Xs); the RS is said to be on a sell signal (or negative) if the most recent signal on the RS chart is a sell signal (a column of Os exceeding a previous column of Os).

In summary, peer RS is one more way to narrow a list of potential buy candidates down to a reasonable number. If a sector suggests that buying can occur within it, you then want to focus on stocks within the sector that exhibit positive peer RS because they will likely be the best performers within that group. ❏

PLAY #36

Compare Your Stocks to the Market—Especially Market Leaders

In horse racing, lame horses stay in the barn, whereas stakes-winning horses get to run in the race.
The same principle holds true in structuring your portfolio.

ONE OF THE THINGS you should do is to periodically review your portfolio and compare the highs and lows of the stocks in it to the highs and lows of the Dow Jones Industrial Average. If the market makes a new high, then you should see your stocks move to new highs as well, or at least be on the verge of new highs. When this does not happen, it is often a sign of impending trouble for that particular stock, a sign of distribution. At the other end, if you have a stock that is making higher bottoms when the Dow is making lower lows, it shows strong demand for that stock and you should hold, or even add to, your positions.

You do not always have to use the Dow to compare, either. If you have a portfolio of secondary stocks, then consider using an index like the Russell 2000. If you have a technology portfolio, then you can use the Nasdaq Composite. If you have a blue-chip portfolio, then you may want to use the Standard & Poor's 500. So you do have choices, depending on the makeup of your portfolio.

As the market moves up, not all stocks go with it. This is certainly not a new revelation. However, selling stocks that have underperformed the market is sometimes difficult. An option strategy that can help in this matter is to sell calls against those positions. Selling calls will bring cash (from the premium) into the account. For this cash, you agree to sell the stock at a particular price. If you sell out-of-the-money calls, then you agree to sell the stock at a higher price. And if you are called away, you remove a stock from your portfolio that is not performing as well as you would like. You also generate cash to enter another position you think will outperform the market.

On the other side, the call could expire worthless. In that case, you keep the call premium you received initially. This makes the position more profitable and more productive than if you had done nothing. ❏

PLAY # 37

Buying on a Pullback

Patience is a virtue.

ONE TACTIC THAT can be used to increase your probability of success is to buy a stock after it has pulled back rather than on the original breakout. This applies to selling short also, by waiting for the stock to rally after breaking down. Below is an example of what we mean by using the long side (**BUYING ON A PULLBACK**, page 102).

As you can see from the chart on the following page, the buy signal occurs at $38, as denoted by the B, and then the stock reverses and pulls back. By waiting for the pullback, you are essentially buying the stock at a discount. Buying on a pullback will improve your gain as well as your performance over the long haul. These pullbacks take place fairly often, so you can be more selective if you choose to be.

Of course, the risk of waiting for a pullback is that you will miss a move. However, there are many, many stocks out there, and missing one here and there will not offset the benefits of regularly waiting for that pullback. We like to use the analogy of the train leaving the station. You may miss that particular train, but if you are patient and wait, another train headed in the same direction will come along. Also, keep in mind that waiting for a pullback will give you

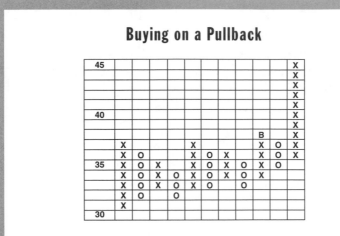

Buying on a Pullback

The "B" represents the buy signal on a spread triple top break. Notice that after moving to 38, the stock then pulls back. This is where you purchase the stock.

a better entry point with an improved risk-reward ratio. In the example above, you purchase the stock at 35 as opposed to 38. This also means you are closer to your stop-loss price, reducing the amount of risk you have in the stock and therefore increasing the potential reward if the stock rallies. While easier said than done, try to exercise some patience and buy your stocks when they come back to you. ❏

PLAY # 38

Momentum

Keep the momentum on your side. When your team
has the momentum, don't call a time-out.

WE USE MEASURES OF momentum and overbought/oversold readings to aid in our interpretation of a stock. The measures are computed by our database and can be accessed by clients. We have three different momentum calculations: daily, weekly, and monthly momentums.

Daily momentum is a very short-term trading tool. Following weekly momentum is very helpful when timing trades as well, but it gives a slightly longer horizon. It is an intermediate tool, since changes to positive or negative weekly momentum last seven weeks on average. The monthly momentum is used more to highlight or signify a longer-term turnaround.

We'll use weekly momentum as an example, but the same principles apply to daily and monthly momentums. Weekly momentum is basically a one-week moving average compared to a five-week moving average. The moving average is also exponentially weighted and smoothed. The exact calculation is proprietary. When the one-week moving average crosses above the five-week, we say the weekly momentum is positive. This would suggest a bounce in the stock. When the one-week moving average crosses below the five-week, we say the weekly momentum is negative. This would suggest a pullback in the stock.

The weekly momentum calculation was created well before computer graphics became as sophisticated as they are today. At that time, it was difficult to draw two lines (the one-week and the five-week) and see where they crossed one another. Therefore, we turned to the actual calculation and created two columns. One column is labeled *top*, which is the positive column, and the other column is labeled *bot*, which is the negative column. As a visual, think of the line between the top and bot columns as the five-week moving average. When the calculation (or the numbers) moves from the bot column to the top column, the one-week has crossed above the five-week. Likewise, when the top column prints zeros and the bot column has a negative calculation, the one-week has crossed below the five-week moving average. The same premise applies to the daily and monthly calculations. It is simply a different time frame.

Momentum calculations are used as a supplement, not a substitution for, the point and figure chart. When we get down to evaluating the individual stock chart, the three most important parts are the relative strength, trend, and the individual patterns. Once we have determined that those three things are positive, then we look at the short-term timing tools like weekly momentum. Let's say, for

Coca-Cola (KO) Weekly Momentum Table

DATE	TOP	BOTTOM	LAST	CROSS
08/09/00	0.0000	-0.0180	59.813	63.100[1]
08/04/00	0.0050	0.0000	62.125	61.303
07/28/00	0.0090	0.0000	62.688	61.121
07/21/00	0.0170	0.0000	60.688	57.895
07/14/00	0.0240	0.0000	57.625	53.833
07/07/00	0.0290	0.0000	58.750	54.176
06/30/00	0.0210	0.0000	57.438	54.009
06/23/00	0.0540	0.0000	57.875	49.734
06/16/00	0.0360	0.0000	55.500	50.116
06/09/00	0.0620	0.0000	52.313	43.614
06/02/00	0.0700	0.0000	52.563	42.747
05/26/00	0.0710	0.0000	54.563	44.524
05/19/00	0.0690	0.0000	50.063	40.643
05/12/00	0.0800	0.0000	52.250	41.356
05/05/00	0.0430	0.0000	47.063	41.222
04/28/00	0.0480	0.0000	47.063	40.416
04/21/00	0.0540	0.0000	49.438	41.923
04/14/00	0.0530	0.0000	46.875	39.652
04/07/00	0.0150	0.0000	46.250	44.090
03/31/00	0.0150	0.0000	46.938	44.681[2]
03/24/00	0.0000	-0.0140	47.000	49.167
03/17/00	0.0000	-0.0400	49.125	55.853
03/10/00	0.0000	-0.0750	44.813	57.799
03/03/00	0.0000	-0.0720	49.938	62.911
02/25/00	0.0000	-0.1120	48.688	70.470
02/18/00	0.0000	-0.0680	51.375	63.726
02/11/00	0.0000	-0.0380	55.313	62.132
02/04/00	0.0000	-0.0170	56.375	59.478
01/28/00	0.0000	-0.0100	56.938	58.800[3]
01/21/00	0.0140	0.0000	66.875	64.306

[1] Weekly momentum turns negative
[2] Weekly momentum turns positive
[3] Weekly momentum turns negative

example, that we have a stock that is bullish on everything, but the weekly momentum has flipped negative. That suggests we put in our order for new positions on a pullback. Again, the momentum doesn't change our opinion of the stock, but rather it helps us time the trade.

The charting and database system on our Web site allows you to actually pull up the table for weekly momentum, and it also tells you where the momentum would change (the cross point). For example, a stock trading at $73 may have negative weekly momentum and a cross point of $75. That would tell us the stock would have to rise to $75 to turn to positive weekly momentum. If the stock didn't rise to $75 at the end of that week, then a new calculation is done and that cross point may have changed. Remember, you are looking at a one-week versus five-week moving average, so each week you are dropping off a week and picking up a new one in your calculation.

Also, on our system you can search for stocks with positive or negative momentum and see how long those momentums have been positive or negative. One of our favorite searches on the system is to look for stocks that have positive trend charts and positive relative strength, but have had negative weekly momentum for twelve weeks or more. The reason for the positive trend chart and positive relative strength chart is to get a stock with an overall upward bias.

We look for weekly momentum that has been negative for twelve weeks or more for two reasons. First, if momentum has been negative for twelve weeks or more, the stock is likely to be on a pullback, thus giving us a stock in an overall positive trend that is on a pullback. Second, we choose twelve weeks or more because the average time momentum stays on the positive or negative side is six to eight weeks. At twelve weeks on the negative side, that is getting "long in the tooth," and a change to positive momentum is likely just at hand. Therefore, we are getting a long-term positive stock, which has pulled back short-term, but is getting ready to start moving again (COCA-COLA (KO) WEEKLY MOMENTUM TABLE). ❏

Using Pre- and Post-Split Charts

It now has become commonplace for stocks to split. In fact, some have split more than once in a single year. This phenomenon is accounted for in the point and figure charting process.

AGAIN, POINT AND FIGURE charting is based on the battle between supply and demand. The charts depict this battle using Xs to signify demand and Os to signify supply. Support and resistance areas are easily seen on the charts. Support is formed when enough

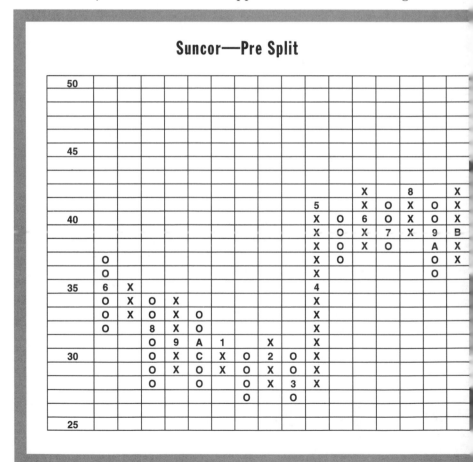

Suncor—Pre Split

demand enters the picture to cause the Os to stop falling, and resistance is formed when enough supply shows up to cause the Xs to stop rising.

What happens when a stock splits, and how are these support and resistance levels portrayed in the post-split chart?

Typically, when a company splits its stock, it will do so in increments like two for one or three for two. A two for one split would indicate that holders will receive two shares for every one they currently have. Since you would have two times as many shares, the price of the stock would be cut in half. In these cases, the price history of the stock would also be adjusted for the split. So if XYZ splits two for one, we would divide the historical data by two to adjust for

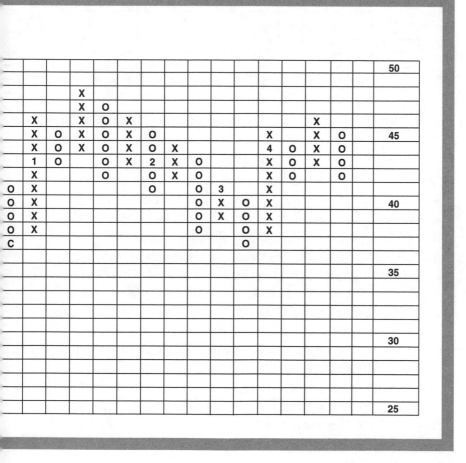

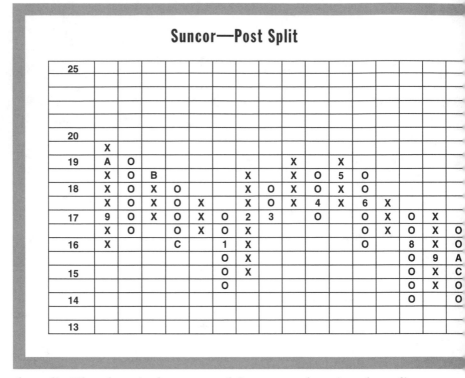

the split. The chart is then created from scratch, using the split-adjusted data.

It is important to look at the post-split chart as soon as possible after the split is announced, especially if you are about to initiate a position or stop out of one. The post-split chart can sometimes look different after the split. Often after splitting the data and re-charting, the chart will lose some of the reversals that the pre-split chart had. In essence, the split chart comes out looking a bit more extended, or with fewer columns. If a stock is at 73 in a column of Xs and then sells off to 70, causing a reversal down into a column of Os, how would that play out in a chart that is split two for one? After splitting the data, we would find the stock up to 36 in Xs (73/2=36.5). The low price of 70 would be 35 after the split adjustment, and that is not enough to reverse the post-split chart. These situations have the potential to make the split chart look different.

If you own a company that has announced a split, be sure to evaluate the post-split chart. In some cases, that chart can show

```
                                                  25
                              X
                              X   O   X
                              1   O   4
                X       8       X   X   O   X     20
          X     6   O   X   O   X   O   X   2   X
          X   O X   O   X   O   B   O   X   O   X
          X   O X   7   A   X   O   X   O   X      19
          X   5         O       X   C       3
          X             O                          18
          4
          X                                        17
          X
          X                                        16
1     X       X
X  O  2  O    X                                    15
X  O  X  O    X
   O  X  3    X                                    14
   O     O
                                                   13
```

that you need to give it a little bit more room than you otherwise would. Take the example of Suncor (SU) in the charts above and on pages 106–107. The pre-split chart shows that the stock had made a series of lower tops and bottoms, and it eventually violated the bullish support line. This violation of the support line changed the trend from positive to negative, suggesting that supply was in control. As it turns out, the pre-split chart created a bearish signal reversed pattern, and in March, it violated the bearish resistance line, changing the trend back to positive. If you had also consulted the post-split chart from February forward, you would see that the stock pulled back from a January high, but held support in March at 18½, above the bullish support line. Using the post-split chart might have convinced you to give Suncor extra room, using the violation of the support line as a stop-loss point. This may have kept you in the stock (**SUNCOR—PRE SPLIT** and **SUN-COR—POST SPLIT**). ❑

Insider Buying vs. Insider Selling

The advent of the Internet has provided easier access
to a valuable source of information—insider buying
and selling. Combining the activity of company officials
with the point and figure chart can give you an extra
edge in the analysis of that issue.

INSIDERS ARE NO DIFFERENT from anyone else. They buy
stock in their company because they believe it will move higher in
price, not lower. Insiders are not right all the time, but they are as
close to the company as you can get. If the company is having a difficult time fundamentally, stockholders within the company are the
most likely to know it and will not buy the stock. Whether someone is an insider or not, the motivation to buy the stock is the same:
a desire to see its value increase. Therefore, take note when insiders buy. Often they are early, but if you find a stock with high insider buying, then people very close to the company believe strongly
in it and have cast their votes in favor of the company with their
own money. That is the most powerful fundamentalist vote around.
Also, look for more than just one buyer. One insider might be new
to the company or just misinformed, but a larger number of insiders are not as likely to be.

Insider selling is a different matter. There are many reasons
insiders might choose to sell stock, and it might have nothing to
do with their outlook for the company. They might need to diversify their portfolio or maybe they are buying a new house. Don't
be overly concerned if an insider sells. However, a large number
of insiders selling stock is worthy of concern. When they are all
jumping ship and the chart suggests supply is in control, you do
not want to be the one going down with the ship.

Use the insider activity as an additional criterion to help make
your investment decisions. Finding the insider activity on a stock is
easy, especially with the sources now available on the Internet. We
can pull up a P&F chart and be within two clicks of a summary of

what firms like the stock on a fundamental basis as well as any recent insider activity. If you find a company that the analyst believes is fundamentally sound, and the insiders have agreed by buying stock, then watch for the point and figure chart to confirm that demand is in control, indicating a time to buy. ❑

The Quality of the Merchandise Is Important

Mike Moody, one of our money managers, explains how understanding the resale value of cars is similar to that of stocks, and how it is one of the keys to making money in the stock market.

MOST PEOPLE THINK about resale value only once every few years when they buy or sell a car. Why is it that a Mercedes has great resale value even when it's ten years old, whereas a Yugo sells for the scrap value of the metal? Clearly, the Mercedes is a better vehicle, safer, and something of enduring quality that people place a value on long after it is new. In fact, most people would rather own a used Mercedes than a new Yugo.

The stock market operates on exactly the same principle. Your portfolio is nothing more than inventory to be bought and sold, the same as if the stocks were used cars or toys. Your job is to buy cheaply, mark up the merchandise, and resell it. The quality of the merchandise is the important factor. Not only does what you buy have to be cheap, but also, there has to be some prospect of people wanting it later at a higher price. Basically, you want to buy Mercedes-caliber merchandise because people always want it later. You can get a great deal on a truckload of hula hoops, but it doesn't much matter how cheaply you buy them if they sit in your warehouse because no one wants them.

Certainly there is a place in some portfolios for the speculative flyer, the occasional trade, and the IPO, but in managing accounts, pay close attention to the quality and reputation of the stocks that are purchased.

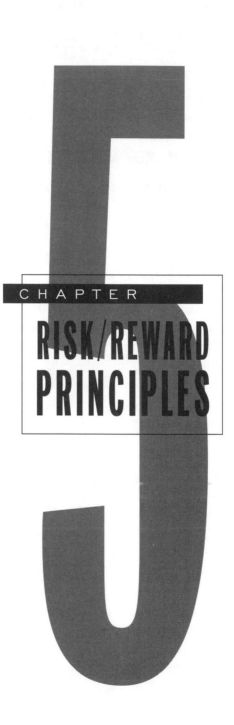

RISK/REWARD PRINCIPLES

COACHES AND PLAYERS ALIKE prepare for the game by watching films and sending out scouts. This is all in an effort to size up their opponents and identify their strengths and weaknesses. Likewise, the market is a formidable opponent and one not to take lightly. Understanding sound risk/reward principles will help you size up the market as an opponent. The following strategies will help you score often, while attempting to reduce your losses.

PLAY #42

A Free Lunch—Not:
Higher Returns Come with Higher Risk

Volatility is the price you pay for higher returns. We get a lot of calls in money management when the market gets choppy or declines, because we have a reputation for being willing to play defense when the market dictates. Invariably, the calls go something like this: "Well, the other manager had great numbers the last couple of years, but this year they just blew up."

THERE IS A BASIC misunderstanding at work here: the belief in the free lunch. The back-to-back 50+ percent years the manager just had do have a cost. Now that the manager is down 50 percent this year, you've just been given the bill.

Volatility is the price you pay for higher returns. On the plus side, this is why stocks earn more than bonds and cash over long stretches of time; people who can handle the volatility get paid for it. On the negative side, this is why high returns are inseparable from high risk, despite what the manager may say. Does anyone remember the low-risk mortgage funds of 1993? The low-risk world dollar funds of 1994? The "market-neutral" hedge funds of late? They all did poorly in the end.

When high volatility surfaces, not only do investors panic in droves, but the wide swings can kill the returns, too. For example, the three-year return of a fund that has back-to-back 50+ percent years, but that is down 50 percent this year, is about 4 percent annually! (Many hedge funds will be lucky to have numbers that good.) We will entertain any and all free lunch offers, but so far we have not found one that doesn't come with indigestion. ❏

Evaluating Risk/Reward
When Initiating New Positions

Risk/reward analysis is a very important component
of stock selection. Such analysis helps to identify the
potential return in a given stock compared to the amount
of risk taken. Ideally, you want at least a two-to-one ratio—
two points of profit for every one point of risk.

RISK/REWARD IS just what the name implies. It is the
process of evaluating how much risk you will take on compared to
how much reward you can expect to gain on any given trade. Or
said another way, how many points could the stock fall if the trade
doesn't work out, versus how many points could the stock rise if
the trade does in fact go in your favor? Typically, when evaluating
risk/reward, we like to see a two-to-one ratio, at a minimum. In
other words, for every point of risk, we want to have two points of
potential reward.

So, as the above suggests, you need to be able to determine the
expected reward and the potential risk. How do you do that? Well,
a few things are needed to calculate the amount of risk versus
reward.

◆ Determine where significant resistance lies ahead, or where the
stock would be overbought on its trading band.

◆ Determine where significant support resides below.

◆ Calculate the price objective for the stock, using either the vertical or horizontal count.

◆ Determine one's stop-loss point—where the stock will break a
significant bottom or trendline, the point at which you no longer
want to own the stock. You must be able to handle the worst-case
scenario—that of the trade not working, and therefore being
stopped out.

We also want to mention that market and sector risk should not
be ignored. Of course, you still need to narrow down the list of

potential buy candidates by focusing on strong stocks in strong sectors. But once the list has been vastly narrowed, then a risk/reward analysis on each stock must be conducted. So now let's go through a couple of examples of evaluating risk/reward using XYZ Technology (XYZ), below.

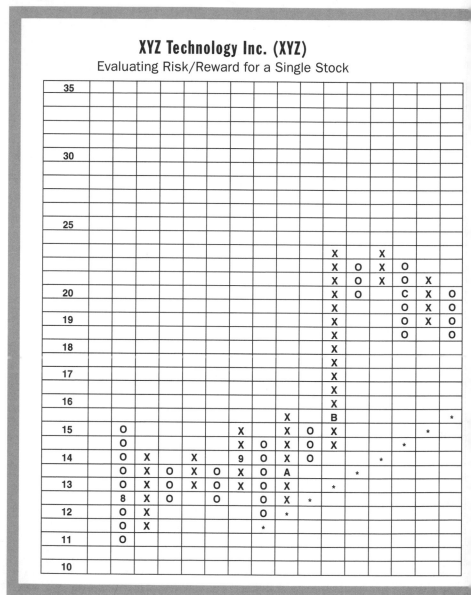

XYZ Technology Inc. (XYZ)

Evaluating Risk/Reward for a Single Stock

EXAMPLE ONE

XYZ TECHNOLOGY HAS rallied up to 33, breaking a double top at 29 after finding support at 21. The stock has rallied to a new high and has no overhead resistance. The (incomplete) bullish price objective is 58. The stop-loss point is 19½, which would be a viola-

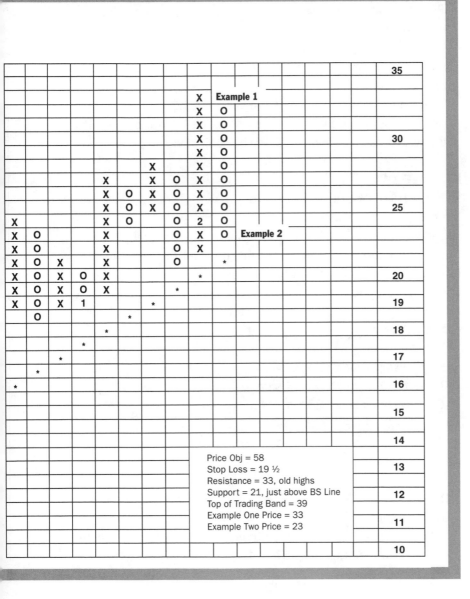

tion of the bullish support line; 18 could have been chosen as a stop, as that would break a spread quadruple bottom. Let's say this stock is in a group that continues to exhibit good relative strength versus the market. Support lies at 20 to 21 initially, then 18½. The top of the ten-week trading band is 39.

Risk/reward calculation
Reward=25 points to the upside
(58 price objective – 33 current price)
Risk=13½ points to the downside
(33 current price – 19½ initial stop-loss point)
Risk/reward ratio=25 points reward / 13.5 risk=1.85 to 1
(this ratio would be worse if you use the 18 stop, or used the top of the trading band at 39 as your objective)

EXAMPLE TWO

XYZ TECHNOLOGY RALLIED up to a new high of 33, then pulled back to 23. It remains on a double-top buy signal and has initial support at 20 to 21; below that is notable support at 18½. There is minor overhead resistance at 33 and the top of the ten-week trading band is 39. The bullish price objective is 58, using a vertical count. The stop loss point is 19½, which would be a violation of the bullish support line. Those longer-term in nature can choose to use 18 as the stop point.

Risk/reward calculation
Reward=35 points to the upside
(58 price objective – 23 current price)
Risk=3½ points to the downside
(23 current price – 19½ initial stop loss point)
Risk/reward ratio=35 points reward / 3½ points risk=10.0 to 1

Risk/reward if you use either 33 initial resistance, or 39 top of trading band:
Ratio=10 points reward / 3½ points risk=2.85 to 1, or 16 points reward / 3½ points risk=4.57 to 1

So as you can see, buying XYZ Technology on a pullback great-ly improved your risk/reward situation. Buying this stock as laid out in Example One was unacceptable on a risk/reward basis, but buying this stock as laid out in Example Two was very attractive on a risk/reward basis, even if only looking to trade it back up to the initial resistance of 33. When you are going through and trying to decide which stocks to buy and where, be sure to evaluate the risk/reward characteristics. It is a very important component to overall success in the stock market. This is especially true when the market is experiencing great volatility and choppiness. Be willing to wait for that stock you want to buy to pull back closer to support. As you can see, by waiting for a pullback, you greatly improve the "reward" part of the equation and reduce the "risk"! (XYZ TECHNOL-OGY INC (XYZ)). ❏

PLAY #44

Catching a Falling Knife

Understanding how support levels are developed increases
your chances of buying a stock that is ready to rebound
versus buying a stock just starting a spiraling descent.

I'M SURE YOU HAVE SEEN the elaborate tricks magicians and movie stuntmen perform with knives. They throw them at tar-gets with amazing accuracy, dodge oncoming knives with incredi-ble speed, and stop hurling knives with their bare hands without so much as a nick. If only investing were so easy.

Many times strong stocks begin to fall in price. How do you determine whether the decline in price is over or just the begin-ning of something much worse to come? We have several ways of determining if a stock is at a support level. Generally once a stock reaches a support level (as discussed below), you will see at least a bounce in the stock, allowing for a slightly better exit point if you're long the stock. In other cases, a stock in a strong uptrend may just be taking a breather and the pullback to support is a buy-ing opportunity.

BULLISH SUPPORT LINE

IN THE POINT AND FIGURE methodology the bullish support line is a line drawn at a 45-degree angle from the lowest point on the chart. The point and figure support line is drawn differently from a bar chart support line. The bar chartist draws a support line that connects the low points on the chart as the stock rises. As long as the stock stays above the bullish support line, we say that the main trend is positive. Bullish support lines can remain in effect for several years, and they often act like brick walls. Stocks that pull back to their bullish support lines are usually good buys as investments and trading opportunities. Not only are you buying the stock more cheaply, but also a violation of the bullish support line affords you a close stop-loss point.

SECTOR IS IN THE "GREEN ZONE"

FOR EACH SECTOR of the market, we measure the percentage of stocks within that group that are on a point and figure buy signal. This percentage is then plotted on a grid from 0 percent to 100 percent. When the percentage falls to 30 percent or below, we say the sector is in the "green zone." Most of the people who want out of that sector have already sold. Sometimes a sector may reach a "green zone" only once every year or so, but a visit to this area of the sector bullish percent chart usually represents a very washed-out condition with limited downside risk.

BOTTOM OF THE TEN-WEEK TRADING BAND

EVERYONE IS FAMILIAR WITH the distribution curve or bell curve concept from Stats 101 class in college. Creating a bell curve entails entering data points into a formula one can construct into a statistical bell curve or a range. The same thing can be done with stocks. We have tweaked the standard bell curve formula a bit to include a volatility calculation and then taken ten weeks' worth of data for any stock and created a bell curve for it. The 100 percent oversold level is three standard deviations below normal. When a stock reaches this level on its chart, it suggests the stock is ready for a bounce back to normal on the curve. If a stock is in an overall downtrend, but reaches the bottom of its ten-week trading band, bounces from that area can be used to exit the stock at a better price. If a stock is in an overall uptrend, pullbacks to the bottom of the ten-week trading band are excellent buying opportunities.

CHART SUPPORT

ONE OF THE BEAUTIES of a point and figure chart is that the patterns are so easily discernible. For instance, one can pull up charts of any number of stocks and see that they create levels where support can be found. In strong relative strength stocks, these support levels are usually areas to which the stock previously pulled back before heading higher. In weaker relative strength stocks, they can present trading opportunities for a bounce to resistance. ❑

PLAY #45

Using Options as a Low-Risk Way to Initiate Positions

Do you pass or run the football? Do you buy stocks or buy calls?
When you are back near your own goal line, it is often prudent
to hand the ball off to your running back rather than throw
a risky pass. Using calls to scale into the market can be an
advantageous way to get yourself back into the football game.

OPTIONS CAN BE a very effective tool for transferring risk from one investor who does not want to take that risk to another who is willing to accept it. There are two good examples of what we mean here, although these are certainly not the only examples. The first arises when the market is falling and fear begins to set in. Investors willing to purchase stocks decide that maybe they should wait a little longer, and they pull their buy orders. With no one willing to step up to the plate and buy, stocks continue to drop. It is in times such as these that good buying opportunities present themselves. Unfortunately, most investors still perceive a great deal of risk in the market and continue to stay away.

Let's look further at this first example. When stocks are falling, the news that investors read in the financial media and see on television is negative. This makes investors pessimistic, and very often they sell the stocks they own, instead of picking up some good stocks at reasonable prices. This is where options come in. Instead of buying a number of stocks, you can invest a small portion of your investment funds and buy a portfolio of calls. This gives you the opportunity to participate in the market, should it advance, without investing a great deal of money. And since you did not invest everything you had, a further decline will not hurt as much.

Make sure you diversify this portfolio and buy calls on stocks from different industry groups. Also make sure you buy options with plenty of time left until expiration. This is not a time to buy "cheap" options, those with only a month or two before expiration. Buy time and give the calls time to work.

Here is what this portfolio of calls does for you:

◆ First, it gets you into the market without requiring a great deal of money. You buy in-the-money calls and use them as stock substitutes. Being in the market means you will not miss a major advance. Since you are buying them as stock substitutes, buy only as many calls as you would round lots of the stock. For example, if you were going to buy 500 shares of a stock, buy only five calls. Don't buy ten or twenty or more calls.

◆ Second, should the market move lower, your losses are limited to the purchase price of the calls. This limits your risk. Of course, these losses can be offset by interest earned from the balance of your funds that are not in the market.

◆ Third, buying a portfolio of calls will give you diversity and will also reduce your risk in case one stock goes against you.

◆ Finally, if the market rallies, you will have a choice of what you want to do with your call positions. You can either take profits in your calls or exercise them and establish equity positions at lower prices.

The second example we want to focus on occurs not when the market is falling, but when it is rising. In this case, everything appears rosy. Earnings reports are good and so are the economic reports. There are invariably investors who may have missed the market and are now willing to get in. More than likely, they want to buy the "hot" stocks, but these are the ones that have rallied the most, more than likely. You can just go out and buy these stocks, but since they have already rallied, the fear in this case is of buying at the top, which means you potentially have a great deal of risk. The good news is, once again, options give you a way to initiate positions with a limited risk: purchasing call options on the stocks you want to buy. By buying calls, your risk is predetermined. You know exactly how much you can lose if the stock or stocks go against you. We mentioned buying a portfolio of calls in the first example. You can do that here as well, and it would spread the risk further.

We mentioned buying only as many calls as you would round lots of the underlying stock. We must reiterate that you should not abuse these strategies. The point is to be able to initiate positions when risk is either very high, or when it is perceived high, and to initiate these positions with a reduced amount of risk. Buying twenty calls when you typically purchase 500 shares is abusing the strategy. If the stock rises, everything works out just fine. However, if the stock declines, you can lose a lot more in the calls than you would have in the stock. You can lose all of your money, in fact. This is when investors say buying calls is a terrible strategy. So be prudent, and remember what you are trying to accomplish. ❏

P L A Y # 4 6

Reducing Risk in a Stock—
Selling It and Buying a Call

Put something away for a rainy day.

THOSE OF YOU WHO have invested in the market for some time have no doubt experienced a rally in the market. Sometimes you are even amazed at how well a specific stock in your portfolio has done. In fact, you are so amazed that you may believe that stock will continue to rise. However, you must remember that until you sell, all you have is a paper profit. While your stock may keep rising, often those very same stocks come back down.

One of the more difficult decisions to make in the market is when to sell. Regardless of when you sell, you almost always second-guess yourself. The thought process you used when you purchased the stock does not appear quite so useful, because you want to make as much as you can. You may even put the question off and try not to answer it, but in most cases you cannot delay for very long. So what we want to know is can this particular stock continue to keep going up and if so, how high? Not only that, but also how can I participate, yet keep my exposure to a minimum?

There is a strategy that may allow you to participate in further gains in the stock while also cutting your risk in it. This strategy is selling your stock and then purchasing a call option on it. Remember that a call allows you to purchase a stock at a given price within a specific period of time. Selling the stock locks in a profit for you. Then you take a portion of the profits and use them to buy the calls. You don't want to go hog-wild here. If you sold 500 shares of the stock, then simply buy five calls. Do not take all of the proceeds and use all of the profits to buy as many calls as you can. Buy only as many calls as you had round lots of the stock. This is how you lock in a profit and save for that rainy day.

Should the stock continue to rally, then the calls will rise and you will still participate in that rally. However, should the stock decline, you can lose only the premium you paid for the calls. Since you only took some of the profits and not all of them, a drop in the stock will reduce your ultimate profit. However, you will still have a profit overall, and if the stock falls sharply, you will be much better off having owned the calls instead of the stock itself. Plus, you will have reduced your risk in the position. ❑

PLAY #47

The Mathematics of Losses

Limit losses and let your winners run.

PSYCHOLOGICALLY, TAKING LOSSES can be a hard thing to do. It means that you must admit the trade didn't work out. People often look at losses as defeat, and admitting defeat is a difficult thing to do. However, one common thread between good traders

Freddie Free-Wheeler's Account

SHARES	BEGIN PRICE	END PRICE	GAIN/(LOSS)
100	$50	$25	($2,500)
100	50	25	(2,500)
100	50	25	(2,500)
100	50	25	(2,500)
100	50	25	(2,500)
100	50	60	1,000
100	50	60	1,000
100	50	60	1,000
100	50	60	1,000
100	50	60	1,000

Gain/(loss) ($7,500)

Deborah Discipline's Account

SHARES	BEGIN PRICE	END PRICE	GAIN/(LOSS)
100	$50	$50	$0
100	50	50	0
100	50	50	0
100	50	45	(500)
100	50	45	(500)
100	50	45	(500)
100	50	45	(500)
100	50	45	(500)
100	50	45	(500)
100	50	45	(500)

Gain/(loss) ($3,500)

and good investors is their ability to limit losses. They are quick to cut their losses short and let their winning positions run. Most people do the exact opposite—they let their losses run and are trigger-happy to take the gains. Let's take a look at a couple of examples of the mathematics of cutting your losses, and maybe next time you have a trade that doesn't go your way, you'll be quicker on the trigger to take the loss.

EXAMPLE ONE

WE HAVE TWO INVESTORS, Freddie Free-Wheeler and Deborah Disciplined. Each starts with a portfolio of ten stocks, 100 shares apiece, and each is priced at $50. Freddie Free-Wheeler doesn't have a sell discipline to limit his losses, whereas Deborah Disciplined does. Let's take a look at each one's portfolio six months after inception. Freddie Free-Wheeler's account shows five stocks down 50 percent and five stocks up 20 percent each. Deborah Discipline's account shows a loss of 10 percent for seven stocks and even for three stocks. Freddie Free-Wheeler's account is down $7,500, while Deborah Discipline's account is down only $3,500. What's more, none of her stocks moved higher, while Freddie Free-Wheeler had 50 percent of his stocks showing nice gains.

If you limit your losses, you can afford to be wrong more often with less of an impact on the portfolio than you would have if you were really wrong a couple of times (**FREDDIE FREE-WHEELER'S ACCOUNT** and **DEBORAH DISCIPLINE'S ACCOUNT,** page 125).

EXAMPLE TWO

STOCKS ARE GOING TO fluctuate back and forth in price, and sometimes when we buy a stock, even though we have done everything we can to stack the odds in our favor, the trade just doesn't work out right away. However, if you let that loss continue to mount and mount, you are creating a mountain instead of a molehill that must be scaled to get back to even. If a stock loses 50 percent of its value, it must double just to get back to even. However, if a stock loses 20 percent of its value, then you only have to see a 25 percent gain to get back to even (**MATHEMATICS OF LOSSES,** right). ❏

Mathematics of Losses

	STOCK A: 50% LOSS	STOCK B: 30% LOSS	STOCK C: 20% LOSS
Original price	$50	$50	$50
After the loss	$25	$35	$40
What it takes to get back to even	100% gain	43% gain	25% gain

PLAY # 48

Stock Insurance—Purchasing Puts to Protect Your Stocks

Pack your parachute in case you need to jump.

OFTEN IN THE MARKET you see a stock that just seems to keep rising. Hopefully, you have experienced this in your own account. Once you have nice gains, though, you begin to wonder if the stock will keep going higher or whether it will begin to decline. One of the things you can do in such a situation is to buy some insurance on your stock. You don't go down to your friendly, neighborhood insurance agent to pick up this insurance. You go to the options market and purchase a put option on that stock.

Many investors have difficulty understanding puts, but they are really quite simple. Anyone who owns a car owns a put. Understanding options is, at its simplest, a matter of understanding the definition of a put and a call. The put simply is a contract giving the buyer the right to sell stock at a certain price and during a certain period. The price is the strike price, and the time period is the expiration date. If you have an accident in your car, you have an insurance policy with an insurance underwriter who states he will pay you the cost of the damage minus the deductible you have. This policy is in force typically for a year until you renew it again. A put is basically the same thing. The only difference is you are insuring against an accident in your stock rather than with your car.

Let's look at an example. We will assume you bought XYZ stock at $50. You could simultaneously buy a six-month-out 50 put for $3. The purchase of the put stipulates you can sell XYZ at $50 anytime before expiration. If XYZ falls all the way to $20, you still have the right to sell at $50.

So what is the risk? It is $3, the cost of the put. If XYZ went bankrupt and declined to zero, you could sell the option for $50, giving you a $47 gain. Of course, you lost $50 in the stock, but your net loss is only $3. You could also exercise the option and sell the stock at $50. All you would lose is the cost of the option ($3). Should the stock rally above $50, you would see the put expire worthless and you would again lose only $3. In the case of the stock rising, though, you continue to participate in the stock's gains, once you have made up the cost of the put. This is a strategy you may want to consider should you see one of your stocks rising rapidly. ❏

SHORT-TERM
TRADING
TECHNIQUES

HAVE YOU EVER NOTICED that the difference in a football game's outcome can often come down to that great special team play or "Hail Mary" pass? The following tips deal with how you can capitalize on special situations in the marketplace. For instance, have you ever taken advantage of option expiration volatility? What about playing a spin-off? Have you ever considered shorting a stock? Using these strategies in your playbook can make you a more well-rounded player and give you a competitive edge.

Tactics for the Short-Term Trader

Becoming an expert short-term trader takes a great deal of work, experience, know-how, and money. It is difficult and can be dangerous. However, you can make good profits by adhering to a strict risk/reward strategy, and these tips should help.

THE NATURE OF THE risk in short-term trading is not understood by very many people. As a trader, you really are not risking your entire investment on a particular transaction, as the odds are high that you will be out of the stock as soon as it looks even remotely weak. The real risk lies in the fact that while a short-term trader cuts his losses, he also cuts his profits. To be successful at this sort of thing, you will have to pick stocks that are going up and going up now. Otherwise, you are going to spend half your fortune and most of your time chasing your tail. Here are some helpful hints:

1 Consider buying after a stock has pulled back. This will give you a better risk/reward ratio and a tighter stop loss. You need every edge in this endeavor.

2 Sell immediately if the stock turns sour. Sell if it drops below its support line. The idea is not to let it head south like a migrating bird. Violation of the support line or a strong area of support is a strong warning to exit the position.

3 Have in mind a fairly precise short-term target. The vertical count used in point and figure would be very effective. If the stock moves up, move the stop loss up below it until you are finally stopped out.

4 An alternative to the above procedures would be to construct a trendline as soon as possible. If this is violated, sell the stock. There is always one main trendline. However, the short-term trader may want to redraw shorter trendlines.

5 Trendlines can prove useful to the short-term trader in another way. A stock in an uptrend may be purchased as it hits the bottom of the trendline. If the stock does not rally off that trendline and continues its decline, then you have a close stop loss. ❑

Bulls Make Money, Bears Make Money, But Pigs Make Nothing

Don't let 1/8 of a point keep you out of a trade.

THE FIRST TIME I heard this expression was while I was working on a bond desk. I had asked a trader for an offering on a large amount of an agency issue. After relaying the offer to the customer, the trader inquired about the status of the trade. I told the trader the customer had passed on his offer, because he was looking for a better price. The trader's response was uncharacteristically tame; he simply said, "Well, bulls make money, and bears make money, but pigs make nothing." I was prepared to hear an earful about how absurd the customer was. Traders can be that way, which is probably why this low-key philosophy stuck in my head.

This brings to mind a couple of thoughts about buying stock. The first is that if you really like a stock and have done the necessary work to support your conclusion, then don't let one-eighth of a point keep you out of the trade. Often investors will put an order in just under the offer, hoping to get a better price, and wind up missing the trade because the stock did not drop that extra one-eighth. Or worse, it really is a stock they want to own, and they end up buying it at a higher price. Unless you are day-trading the issue, if one-eighth or one-quarter is going to make a difference, then maybe you ought to reevaluate the risk/reward parameters of the trade.

The second thought is when to take profits. Consider taking partial profits. Our money managers reduce a position by a third when they are up 30 percent and take another third off when they are up 50 percent. This strategy allows you to take some money off the table. It accommodates reducing risk while allowing the position to run. In addition, reducing the position as it grows helps to keep one stock from becoming too large a percentage of the portfolio. To be successful, it is imperative to let profits run, but be smart as well and protect some of those profits. ❑

Long Tail of Os Down: A Trading Technique

Buying a stock after it reverses up from a long tail of Os down can be a useful trading technique for more aggressive traders.

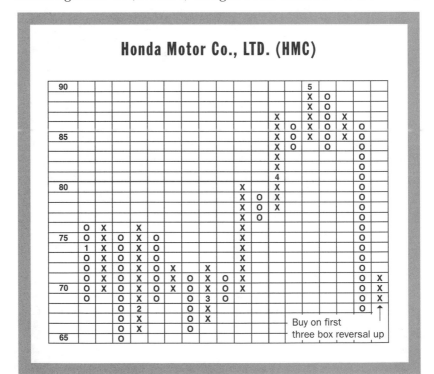 IN THIS DAY AND AGE, investors are always trying to find new ways to "skin a cat," or said another way, to make money in the stock market. One technique we have found useful for the more aggressive trader is playing a stock for a bounce up after it has fallen eighteen Os or more straight down.

More specifically, the aggressive trader identifies a stock that has fallen eighteen Os (or more) straight down on its P&F chart. Then,

Honda Motor Co., LTD. (HMC)

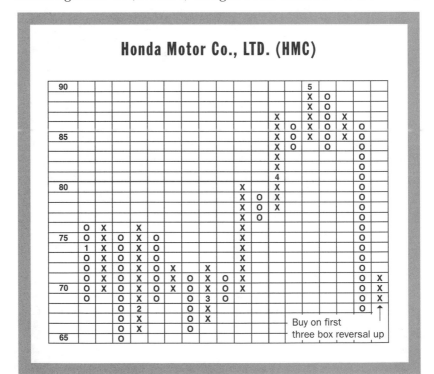

Buy on first three box reversal up

once that stock experiences the first three-box reversal up from that "long tail" down, it can be bought for a trading move back up. The idea here is that a stock quickly drops for whatever reason, then becomes very oversold and is due for a reflex bounce back up. The trader is merely trying to capture this bounce. This type of trade is typically for the more aggressive trader, because usually a stock that has fallen to this degree is in weak hands. In fact, it is often in an overall downtrend—not the type of stock we typically like to recommend. But again, all you are trying to do is play the stock for a bounce.

In playing such stocks, we often like to see that the stock has fallen into some area of previous support from which to bounce back up, and we like to see that the long tail down didn't take a long time to transpire—that it occurred over the course of a few days, not a few weeks or months. We also prefer to see that the stock is oversold on its ten-week trading band.

Again, we wait for the first three-box reversal back up to occur before buying. This reversal up shows that demand is starting to come back into the stock, at least in a short-term respect. The reversal up also serves to set up a stop-loss point—a double-bottom breakdown, should the trade not work out.

In summary, more aggressive traders can buy a stock for a trading move to the upside after it reverses back up from a long tail of Os down. Be sure to adhere to the double-bottom sell signal as your stop point in the event the trade doesn't work out. Also, be willing to take profits if you get a quick move to the upside (**HONDA MOTOR CO., LTD. (HMC)**). ❑

PLAY # 5 2

High Short Interest

Double Demand!! The shorts get squeezed and present you with an upside trading opportunity.

WHEN SEARCHING FOR IDEAS, we often look at the high short-interest ratios that are published each month. The short interest ratio is the number of days it would take, based on average volume, for the outstanding short position to be covered. The higher this ratio, the harder it is for those short to cover and the better the chance for a squeeze. We call it double demand because in order to short a stock, it has to be done on an uptick, which is the first instance of demand.

Once short, the stock will have to be bought back to cover the position, and that is the second form of demand for the stock. If demand retains control of a stock and it moves higher, those who are short "feel the pain" and must decide to cover their position. After all, the risk for the short seller is unlimited; it is not just the price paid for the stock.

So as the pain for those short becomes unbearable, they scramble to buy back the stock. But as they do, it creates additional demand for the stock, and the price rises. As the price rises, it convinces others who are still short, those with more tolerance for pain, that they are wrong, so they cover, creating additional demand. The price continues to rise, and the squeeze gets tighter.

However, there is always the possibility that those who are short are correct, so homework has to be done on both a fundamental and a technical basis. Always have a game plan in place in case the trade goes against you, and know where you plan to stop out. The good thing about the chart is that if the shorts prove to be right, it will be clearly pointed out with sell signals. ❑

PLAY #53

The Selling Climax

The selling climax can signal that a stock has made
an intermediate-term bottom. Such a climax can provide
a reason to "bottom fish" a beaten-up stock.

THE SELLING CLIMAX, which was introduced to us by Mike Burke, occurs when a stock makes a new yearly low (52-week) during the week, then closes up for the week. Such action in a stock suggests that the selling pressure has reached a climactic level; when it makes the new yearly low, then it has likely dried up. When such a selling climax occurs, it often can signal that a bottom has been made in the stock. For those more aggressive in nature, this climax can provide a buying opportunity.

Let's look at an actual example of a selling climax, using our old favorite, XYZ Corp.

XYZ Weekly Price Data

WEEK ENDING	CLOSE	HIGH	LOW	
3/24/00	63.00	63.50	56.75	
3/17/00	57.63	60.50	**51.38**	→ New 52-Week Low
3/10/00	53.75	78.50	52.75	

From the above data, you can see that during the week of March 17, XYZ made a new 52-week low of 51.38. But notice that the stock closed at 57.63, up from the previous week's closing price of 53.75. This is the "Selling Climax," and it suggests the stock could be making an intermediate-term bottom. ❑

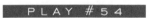

Spin-offs

Watch for spin-offs to move from supply's hands
to demand's hands for a buying opportunity.

SPIN-OFFS USUALLY OCCUR when a company decides that a segment of its business does not meet its primary business focus. The company concludes that it can create greater value for the stockholder by spinning off this segment of the business. Time usually proves them correct, but it is interesting to note that these spin-offs typically underperform the averages during the first three to six months of independent operation. Selling pressure initially comes into play for numerous reasons. It may be that the stock has no fundamental coverage, is not in the S&P 500, and does not have a large capitalization, so managers must sell the issue. However, when the initial selling pressure abates, they typically outperform the averages over the next thirty months.

This is where the point and figure charts can be of immense help.

If the issue typically underperforms the averages during the first three to six months, we can use the P&F chart to help us determine when the tide changes. By following the chart, we can watch for the stock to move from supply's hands to demand's. As demand gains control, the chart will start to give buy signals and make higher bottoms. This will be an indication that the supply has dried up and demand has taken control. If you want to play spin-offs, but be sure to give them some time after the initial offering to let the selling pressure work its way out. When the chart shows demand in control, look for an entry point that provides a good risk/reward ratio. ❏

PLAY #55

When the High-Low Reverses up from below 10 Percent

The point and figure methodology not only encompasses long-term indicators but also includes beneficial short-term timing indicators.

ONE OF THE BETTER short-term indicators we use is the High-Low Index on the New York Stock Exchange. The High-Low Index calculates the percentage of stocks that are hitting new highs versus those making new highs and lows. Said in another way, we calculate the High-Low by dividing the number of stocks hitting new highs by the number hitting new highs and new lows. Once we have this daily reading, we then track those numbers on a ten-day moving average basis.

Upside reversals from below 30 percent are generally considered buy signals. A move down to 30 percent or lower shows an oversold market, and the upside reversal shows something positive happening—fewer stocks making new lows. Declines in this indicator below the 10 percent level typically show a washed-out market. Here, too, we wait for the upside reversal in the indicator. We don't try to anticipate and jump the gun. Since we don't see 10 percent very often, and it indicates a very washed-out condition, we feel we can wait for the upside reversal.

As we write this book, we have only seen the High-Low fall below 10 percent three times since 1994. That is an average of once every two years. For your information, these reversals occurred in December 1994, September 1998, and October 1999. Each of these times the upside reversal by the High-Low Index on its chart led to significant upside moves in the market. This does not mean every reversal will be successful, but nevertheless, the probabilities are there to warrant a play to the upside.

You may ask how you can play such a reversal. One way would be to purchase the SPDRs (Standard & Poor's Depositary Receipts), which mirror the S&P 500 Index, or the Dow Diamonds. Another way is to buy index calls. When the High-Low reverses up, then buy calls on one of the market indices, such as the S&P 100 (OEX) or the Major Market Index (XMI) or the Value Line Index (VLE). Consider closing positions if the High-Low moves to overbought territory (above 70 percent) and turns down. These trades may not happen overnight, so make sure you buy enough time. In other words, do not buy options with the next month's expiration. ❏

PLAY # 56

Strategy for Option Expiration

Don't be afraid to let volatility work for you.

OPTION EXPIRATIONS historically have been and still can be volatile. The so-called Triple Witching Expirations have become infamous for their potential volatility. These expirations occur when futures, options on those futures, and equity and index options all expire at the same time. These occur in March, June, September, and December of each year. We would like to present a possible strategy for you to use during such an expiration. This strategy will possibly allow you to buy stocks at a better price or sell at a higher price. Let's take a look at the strategy.

As we mentioned above, Triple Witching Expirations are often volatile, and we see movement in the market both to the upside and to the downside. For those who are trying to buy a particular stock, here is what you can do. You simply place an order to buy that stock a couple of points below its current price. If the market declines sharply, then your stock may fall and hit the price at which you want to purchase it. If so, you have bought a stock you wanted to own at a better price. Nothing wrong with that!

Conversely, suppose you have a stock in your portfolio that you want to sell, not at the current price, but at a couple of points higher. In this case, you place an order to sell the stock a couple of points above the current price. If the market rallies strongly, then you may sell that stock at the desired price.

Of course, you won't get these trades executed every time. You may set your prices too high or too low and not get any executed. But it is an interesting strategy to use, allowing you to take advantage of the volatility that is often in the market during an expiration.

Let's review the four different triple witching months over the past ten years and whether the volatility has resulted in up moves or down moves.

◆ **March.** Only two of the past eleven years showed down weeks during March triple witching. The two down years were 1997 and

Historical Returns on the S&P 500 during Triple Witching Weeks

YEAR	MARCH	JUNE	SEPTEMBER	DECEMBER
2000	+5.0%	+0.5%	−1.9%	−4.2%
1999	+0.4%	+3.8%	−1.2%	+0.3%
1998	+2.9%	+0.2%	+1.1%	+1.8%
1997	−1.2%	+0.6%	+2.9%	−0.7%
1996	+1.3%	+0.1%	+1.0%	+2.8%
1995	+1.2%	+2.3%	+1.9%	−0.2%
1994	+1.0%	even	+0.6%	+2.6%
1993	+0.1%	−0.8%	−0.6%	+0.5%
1992	+1.3%	−1.5%	+0.8%	+1.7%
1991	−0.4%	−1.2%	+1.1%	+0.7%
1990	+1.2%	+1.2%	−1.7%	+1.5%

1991. In the year 1993 the S&P 500 was basically flat. This may also have something to do with the fact that November to April is historically the best time for the market.

◆ **June.** Out of the past eleven years, six showed less than 1 percent change on a week-to-week basis for the S&P 500. The years 1999, 1995, and 1990 were all up more than 1 percent. In 1999, the S&P 500 was up 3.8 percent for the week, and in 1995 the S&P 500 was up 2.3 percent, both big up moves in very strong markets. There were only two years down more than 1 percent on a week-to-week basis, and that was 1991 and 1992.

◆ **September.** Only four out of the past eleven triple witching weeks showed declines. Those years were 2000, 1999, 1993, and 1990, and the year 1993 saw a decline of less than 1 percent. That means seven out of eleven September triple witching weeks were positive. Only one of those weeks was up less than 1 percent, and that was in 1992, when the S&P 500 was up .8 percent for the week.

◆ **December.** Like the March period, triple witching weeks in general have been good for the S&P 500 during December. Only three years showed down weeks during December triple witching, and they were 1995, 1997, and 2000. During 1995 and 1997, the S&P 500 was only down .2 percent and down .7 percent, respectively. The year 2000 saw a pretty good hit for the S&P 500, down 4.2 percent to cap off a very volatile year. (**HISTORICAL RETURNS ON THE S&P 500 DURING TRIPLE WITCHING WEEKS,** at left). ❏

PLAY #57

Guideline for Selling Short

For those willing to play both sides of the market, capitalizing on downward trending markets or stocks, selling short can be a useful investment strategy. We recommend certain guidelines when selecting stocks to short.

IN STACKING THE ODDS in your favor for a given short position, basically we look for the exact opposite technical criteria than we would for a long position. We try to stack as many negatives as possible in our favor, picking those stocks that techni-

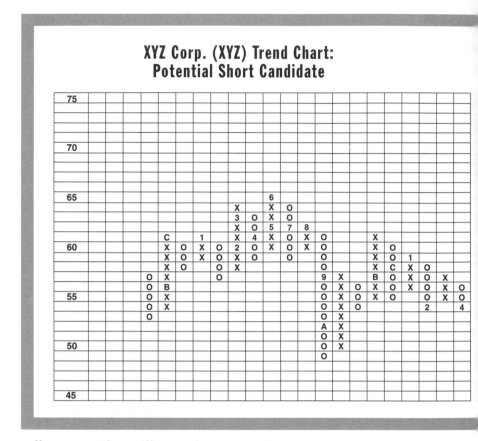

XYZ Corp. (XYZ) Trend Chart: Potential Short Candidate

cally suggest they will move lower in price.

Below we list our ideal criteria for short positions; above is a chart for a stock with some of these traits (**XYZ CORP. (XYZ) TREND CHART: POTENTIAL SHORT CANDIDATE**). You may not have all of these criteria in place, but again, have the weight of the evidence in your favor. Above all, be sure to determine a (buy) stop-loss point and adhere to that stop in the event the trade doesn't work out, as your risk is unlimited if you don't establish that buy stop.

DESIRABLE TECHNICAL CRITERIA FOR SHORT CANDIDATES
◆ Negative Sector Status
◆ Negative Sector RS
◆ Negative overall trend of the stock
◆ Negative Relative Strength (versus market and peers)

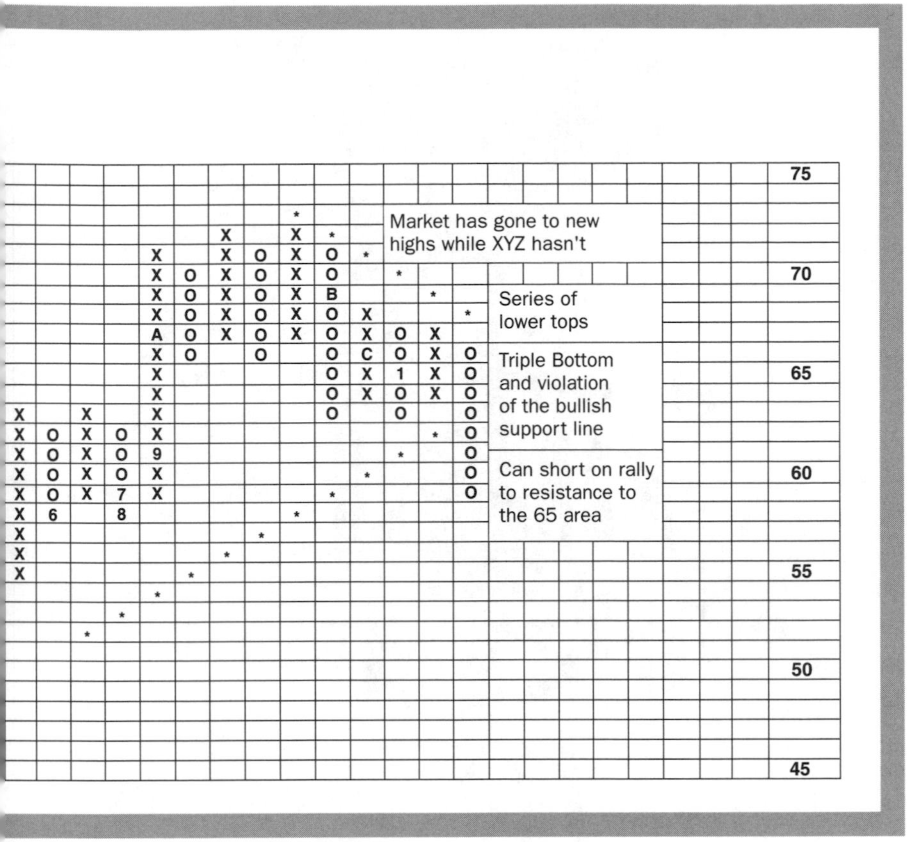

Point-and-figure chart (price levels on right axis: 75, 70, 65, 60, 55, 50, 45) with the following plotted columns and annotations:

													Level
													75
				*									
		X		X	*	Market has gone to new						
	X	X	O	X	O	*	highs while XYZ hasn't					
	X	O	X	O	X	O	*						70
	X	O	X	O	X	B		*	Series of			
	X	O	X	O	X	O	X		*	lower tops		
	A	O	X	O	X	O	X	O	X			
	X	O		O		O	C	O	X	O	Triple Bottom		
	X				O	X	1	X	O	and violation			65
	X				O	X	O	X	O	of the bullish		
X		X		X		O		O		O	support line		
X	O	X	O	X					*	O	Can short on rally		
X	O	X	O	9			*			O	to resistance to		60
X	O	X	O	X				*		O	the 65 area		
X	O	X	7	X			*			O			
X	6		8				*						
X						*							
X				*									55
X			*										
		*											
	*												50
													45

◆ Bearish Chart Pattern

◆ Lower highs

◆ Attractive Risk/Reward (based on bearish price objective and definable stop loss)

◆ Rallied up to notable resistance

◆ Negative Momentum

◆ Rallied up to middle of ten-week trading band ❑

CHAPTER

MANAGING YOUR INVESTMENT

THE CLOCK IS TICKING; it's the fourth quarter. Your football team is winning by a touchdown. The game plan for this particular Sunday has worked out great, despite your formidable opponent. Then, all of a sudden, your quarterback goes down with an injury. Now you must adapt.

The stock market can inflict similar injuries upon you. In managing a portfolio, the market is an opponent that never stops playing the game and will constantly challenge your ability to adapt. The following tips will provide you with strategies to conquer potential setbacks on a consistent basis.

PLAY #58

The Tortoise and the Hare

Over time, managing your money so that you have consistent returns each year will yield better results than huge gains one year and terrible losses the next year.

MORE TIMES THAN WE care to think, we hear the question, "So how did you do this year compared to the S&P 500?" A better question would be "So how has your portfolio performed over the last five years?" Over time, and not even a very long period, consistent results tend to beat the results of a high-risk, high-flying method of stock investing.

To illustrate this, let's take a look at two managers. Manager 1 adheres to the principles of limiting losses and preserving capital in the account. He may give up some opportunity, but that's OK over the long haul. Manager 2, on the other hand, is a highflier. She likes to move and groove, taking a lot of risk. Sometimes she gets the big gain, but on the other hand, sometimes she gets the big loss.

The first year both managers perform the same, but after that we see a big divergence. Manager 1 is controlling risk and making nice returns, but not necessarily knocking the cover off the ball.

		MANAGER 1		MANAGER 2
Start with		$100,000		$100,000
Year 1	12%	112,000	12%	112,000
Year 2	18	132,160	40	156,800
Year 3	22	161,235	45	227,360
Year 4	12	180,583	-5	215,992
Year 5	2	184,195	-33	144,714

Manager 2 is slicing and dicing and making some good returns in years two and three. In years four and five, it's a bit tougher. Sometimes the market has the ball, and sometimes we have the ball. Manager 1 knows the importance of limiting losses. In years four and five, Manager 1 was using risk management tools. Manager 2 doesn't fare nearly as well because risk is a double-edged sword. All of those gains made in years two and three are given back.

If you are managing your account like Manager 1, then you are able to sleep at night, whereas if you're like Manager 2, you're likely to have insomnia. Most of the time the investing public looks at historical returns and jumps on the bandwagon with Manager 2 after year three and becomes disappointed with later returns. ❑

Two Heads Are Better Than One

Often it makes sense to buy a package of stocks within
a particular sector to participate in a move in that group.

HAVE YOU EVER done your homework on a sector and really believed that the group was going to start moving, but the stock you chose didn't participate with the rest of the group? I'm sure that has happened to more than one of you. And you don't have to pick an obscure, no-name stock to have this happen. Let's look at a couple of examples.

From September 1999 until the end of April 2000, the CBOE Software Sector (CWX) was up 48 percent, but Microsoft (MSFT), the stalwart of the sector, was actually down, falling from 92 to 70. So here was the biggest stock in the group, and had you bought Microsoft as your sector proxy for software, you would have missed out on a great move in the sector. Had you been in Oracle (ORCL), you would have been up 251 percent!

But because Microsoft had its lawsuit by the government around its neck, the stock did not participate with the group move. There wouldn't have necessarily been anything wrong with your decision-making to use Microsoft as your proxy stock for that sector—it is one of the largest capitalized stocks out there, but it just didn't participate this time.

This is not an isolated example. For instance, from August 1999 to February 2000 the CBOE Internet Index (INX) was up 70.4 percent, but America Online was only up 29 percent. Clearly this stock was up, but nowhere near the performance for the rest of the stocks in the group.

Remember 1998, when the drug sector was extremely strong? During that time, the Amex Drug Index (DRG) was up 46 percent, and some of the big name stocks did better than others. Pfizer (PFE) was up 68 percent, and Warner Lambert (WLA) was up 82 percent, but Eli Lilly (LLY) was up only 27.7 percent. So again, if you had bought Eli Lilly, you participated, but certainly not to the extent of many of the other names in the group.

How do you solve this problem? One way is to buy a package of stocks within a particular sector. If we like a sector, we may buy two or three names in that group. A recent example is in the retail sector. When the retail relative strength chart reversed up into a column of Xs, we divided our allocation of money for retail between three stocks: Wal-Mart (WMT), Home Depot (HD), and Target (TGT). Wal-Mart and Home Depot did much better than Target, so the account as a whole was better off than if we had made the decision to buy just Target. When the retail relative strength chart reversed down into Os, we wanted to cut back our exposure in that sector. Each of the three charts was examined and Home Depot had the strongest technicals at that time, so we sold Wal-Mart and Target.

Another way to get exposure to a whole sector with just one purchase is the new commoditized sector indices. Merrill Lynch and Barclays have introduced several Holders Trusts and iShares. These trusts are much like the S&P 500 SPDRs that trade on the AMEX. These trusts allow you to buy a package of, let's say, biotech (BBH) stocks, with just one transaction. There are several of these trusts currently available, such as Telecommunications, B2B (BHH), Internet (HHH), and Pharmaceuticals (PPH), with many more in the works. These trusts are another way to participate in a group move without having to pick just one stock. ❏

PLAY # 6 O

Keeping Turnover to a Minimum

The one thing all winners of a Nascar race will tell you is that
they drove a straighter line than anybody else. Investing is
the same way. Try to make as few lane changes as possible.

WE'VE ALL BEEN THERE BEFORE — driving down the highway, late for an appointment. We speed up, exceeding the speed limit to try to make up some time. We pass the guy in front of us who seems to be out for a Sunday afternoon drive. Just as you start thinking, "I'm on my way now," the light turns red and the guy out for a Sunday drive pulls up right next to us. All of that zig-zagging in and out of traffic and driving above the speed limit did nothing to get us there sooner. It only increased our risk of having an accident or getting a ticket.

Our philosophy for investing is that we want to drive as straight a line as possible. We want to make as few moves as possible to get us to our goal. We receive many calls each week asking, "I was thinking about switching into ABC from XYZ. What do you think?" First we look at the chart of XYZ. If everything looks good from a technical standpoint, let that strong horse keep running the race. Even if ABC looks good, unless there is a compelling reason to sell XYZ, stay with it.

An interesting study by Terrance Odean and Brad M. Barber at the University of California-Davis found "Those who trade the most realize, by far, the worst performance." Their study focused on 1,607 investors who switched from phone-based trading to online trading from January 1992 until December 1995. Four basic themes were revealed in this study: "Traders had unusually strong performance before going online; they accelerated their trading after going online; they traded more speculatively after they had Internet access; and they had subpar performance (from accelerated trading) as a result."

We bought Amgen (AMGN) when the biotechnology sector reversed up on its relative strength chart and its sector bullish percent chart was washed out and in the green zone. We purchased the stock around $44, when it was just plodding along, making slow but sure progress. Every day we would see these other biotechnology companies up 20 percent or more in a day, so we started to get "ants in our pants," wanting to take that AMGN position off and switch the symbol into something that really had the ability to move around.

We resisted the urge to do that, and it's a good thing. The biotech sector started to get hit on news that the government was going to have its hand in any DNA mapping that happened, and that was the beginning of the sector getting taken to task. Although Amgen sold off, it didn't sell off nearly as badly as some stocks. The chart continued to hold key support areas, and lo and behold, Amgen started to move a couple of weeks later. It is at a new high now, while many other names are struggling to get back to being down only 50 percent.

A great example is Hyseq (HYSQ). Here is a stock that rallied from the teens to 139, only to fall back to the teens and then recover to the forties. That stock really had the ability to move up and down. HYSQ is that driver you see speeding and weaving down the highway, and you just know he's going to crash. He may get there ten minutes faster, but is the risk of crashing really worth it? For us, it's not. We'd rather stick with the stock that goes the speed limit. That way, the speed bumps that come along on this investment journey (and don't worry; they always do) are easier to handle, and we can still sleep at night. ❏

PLAY # 6 1

Let Profits Run, Not Losses

Most investors measure themselves against the performance of various indices. It's hard enough to be successful at investing, but when you get a winner and cap its potential, it's just about impossible to be successful against these indices.

IN 1999 THE PERFORMANCE of the Nasdaq was envied by all, as the index was up over 100 percent. Indices do not cap gains. In fact, with cap-weighted indices, the stronger the stock, the higher the weight becomes. Indices do not cut losses, either, but the weights do work in favor of the index. The weaker the stock, the smaller the weighting.

The task of letting profits run is much harder than it sounds. However, being able to accomplish this simple-sounding task is imperative to successful investing. A large part of the difficulty in managing a trade that lets the profits run is that we are emotional in our decisions. Letting the profits run requires that we take the emotion out of the trade. It is exciting to buy a stock and have it run up 30 percent in just a matter of weeks. It's a great feeling, and the natural thought is to sell it before supply gains control and the stock drops. The fact is that the really strong stocks tend to remain the strongest. True, they consolidate, pull back, and sometimes give sell signals. However, relative to the market, they typically continue to outperform for an extended period of time.

Don't sell a stock just because it has been strong. If you did that, you may have sold Qualcom (QCOM) in 1999 when it was up 300 percent in about three and a half months. A great return, but you would have left another 735 percent on the table.

Emotion also plays a role in letting losses run. As much as it is a great feeling to see a trade succeed, it is a bad feeling to see one fail, but it happens to all of us. We do our homework and conclude that a stock should move higher, and then it doesn't. Admitting defeat can be the hardest thing to do. We become loyal and attached to the stock. However, by not stopping the bleeding, you severely cripple your chances of being successful. Taking a loss of 15 percent to 20 percent is manageable. Taking a loss of 50 percent is devastating. It's not easy finding stocks that double, and that's what you have to do in order to get back to even after a 50 percent loss. It is imperative that you can call a dog a dog and remove it from your portfolio before it bites you.

Using the tools available with the point and figure methodology can help identify the stocks that will fly and those without the wings to do so. The stocks that are the strongest will have positive relative strength against their peers as well as the market. They will also trade above their bullish support lines, indicating a positive trend. Watch out for those that have proven you wrong. They will likely reverse or give a sell signal on their relative strength chart, and they will violate the bullish support line, changing the trend to negative. Don't be asleep at the switch! ❏

Benefits of Position Sizing for Traders: Percent Risk Method

When managing your portfolio there are several methods to use to determine how many shares to buy for any given trade. One way that we have found beneficial is the percent risk method. This means we size our trading positions based on each trade, risking 1 percent of the total equity in the portfolio. The share size is decided specifically by the distance to the stop-loss point.

ONE VERY IMPORTANT ASPECT of any portfolio is position sizing. Once you decide to make a trade, and you are sure that you have a reasonable stop-loss point as well as a bullish price objective, what happens when you have to decide how much to buy? Does it really matter? Of course it does, and you need to have some rational method of sizing your positions before you even consider a trading portfolio. So here is how we size positions in our tracking portfolio:

We use positions that are based on risk tolerance, or a percent risk model. Let's say you are ready to open a $1 million marginable trading account. Depending on your risk tolerance, you may choose to size your positions equally, based upon a dedicated risk relative to your overall account. For instance, we chose a 1 percent risk tolerance on a portfolio of that size. This means that each position will be sized so that the risk is no more than 1 percent of our $1 million account. One percent of $1 million is $10,000, so that will be our risk for our first position.

So let's now approach that single position based on our calculated risk. In this example, we will use our old favorite, XYZ. Since we can determine our stop-loss point for our trade in stock XYZ, we determine the distance from our entry point to our stop-loss point—the risk to the stop, and then divide that into the $10,000 amount we are willing to risk for the position. The resulting value will be the number of shares that we can purchase to stay within our 1 percent risk tolerance.

Here's an example. XYZ recently completed a three-box reversal up to begin a shakeout pattern at $50 on its trend chart, so we want to buy this stock. We will maintain a stop loss of $45 for traders, which will break a double bottom negating the shakeout, and the stock has opened this morning at $49. So our entry price right now would be $49, and our risk on this trade is $4 ($49 - $45). We now divide our $10,000 risk for this position by our $4 risk per share to give us a lot of 2,500 shares. Naturally, as the distance to your stop-loss point decreases, your share purchase will increase; likewise, the opposite will occur when you are considering stocks trading further from your stop point.

This method of position sizing increases the bet as our equity increases. This is opposed to a martingale strategy, whereby a bet would increase to compensate for losses in a portfolio. Our anti-martingale approach allows our position sizes to increase as our portfolio grows. Let's say our portfolio began at $1 million but after a year of trading was now valued at $1.5 million total equity. Well, using the same position sizing technique, our risk for each position would now be $15,000 (1 percent of $1.5 million), while still risking only 1 percent of our overall account per trade. So let's say that a similar trade presented itself with XYZ. Our position size would now have grown to 3,750 shares ($15,000 divided by $4).

So again, with the percent risk model that we use, the most that is ever risked per trade is 1 percent of the account value at the time the trade is made. (So you mark the account to market each day before you can figure out what the 1 percent risk would be.) The main rule to adhere to with this method is that you must respect your stop points. Remember, your position is sized as a function of the risk to the stop point. So if your stop point is hit, you must stop out.

But the beauty of position sizing is how much it can enhance your returns. If you have a large position on because the stop point

AMR Corp. (AMR)

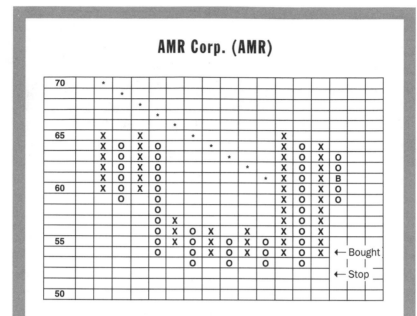

Example of a Trade Using Position Sizing

AMR CORP (AMR)

Price Bought: 54 $\frac{9}{16}$

Stop Point: 52

Risk to Stop= 2 $\frac{9}{16}$

1% of Equity Value= $10,000 (assuming account value of $1 million)

Number of Shares Bought=3,902

Sold at 64 on rally up close to resistance

Profit/Loss on Trade= $36,825.13

BUYING ON A PULLBACK, with a good potential return on the upside, in this case no resistance until the 65 area, provides for an excellent risk/reward situation. I was only risking 2.56 points on the trade with the goal of potentially making a little over 10 points.

is tight, and that trade works out in your favor, it will add considerable money to the bottom line vis-à-vis a smaller position, all the while risking the same as any other trade. An example of this is shown a bit further on.

There are other ways to size your positions, and one would be to make an equi-dollar portfolio, where all trades are of an equal dollar amount, such as buying $100,000 worth of a stock. In the case of the XYZ example, you would buy 2,040 shares. Another method would be to make all of the positions of equal size share allotments, such as buying 2,000 shares of each stock you purchase. We will say, based on research by Van K. Tharp, that the equal share and equal dollar method vastly underperforms the percent risk method.

If you are interested in explanations on other ways to size positions within a portfolio, we recommend purchasing *Trade Your Way to Financial Freedom,* by Van K. Tharp, Ph.D. (McGraw-Hill, 1998). The book has a chapter on position sizing that covers a percent risk model and a percent volatility model, in addition to discussing the limitations of equal-dollar and equal-share models. The percent volatility method sizes positions based on the volatility of the underlying interest. We recommend this book, as it explains very clearly the advantages and disadvantages to particular position sizing techniques. ❑

Extrapolation of Van K. Tharp's Research

IN THARP'S STUDY, the same number of trades/signals were taken regardless of the position sizing model. We have merely summarized the vast difference in returns that can exist as a result of what position sizing model you choose.

MODEL	AMOUNT MADE
Equal Share (Fixed) Amount	$ 237,457
Equal Dollar Amount	231,121
Percent Risk	1,840,493
Percent Volatility	2,109,266

The Hardest Decision Is When to Sell: Taking Profits, Cutting Your Losses, Stop Points, and Trimming

When to sell is probably the hardest part of investing. You punish yourself if you don't stop out and the stock declines, and you kick yourself if you sell the stock, only to watch it go higher and higher. The main thing to remember is that you won't always get in at the absolute bottom, and you will not likely get out at the top. But you must have some type of sell discipline to avoid riding them up and riding them back down. Below we list some points to remember that will help you with the sell decision.

◆ **Taking profits.** When the trade goes in your favor, you must have some type of sell discipline, just as you need one if the trade goes against you. We typically suggest that once you are up 30 percent in a position, you should sell one-third of it to lock in partial profits. This helps you raise cash that can be put to use in another stock, maybe one that is just getting going. It also helps to reduce the size of that position, keeping it more in line with other holdings, thereby not letting one position become too big in a given portfolio.

Should that stock continue to rise, we would then sell a second third once you are up 50 percent. Then we would hold that last third of the position until the technical picture gives signs of serious deterioration, such as a trendline violation or relative strength change. By trimming the position as the stock goes up, but holding a core (original third), you have latitude to hold that last third.

This process can allow you to have stocks that become solid relative-strength performers, ones you may potentially hold for years, such as a General Electric (GE) or Cisco Systems (CSCO). Another benefit of trimming the position, rather than selling it all, is that if you want to come back at a later date and buy that same stock, adding to your position because the fundamentals and technicals suggest you do so, you will be more likely to if you already have a core position.

Think about it. How many of you owned Microsoft (MSFT) years ago, only to sell it and take a nice profit? How many of you went back into it? Or did you not want to buy it again when it was higher than when you sold it? Microsoft was only up 9,570 percent in the 1990s. Trimming it, not selling it all, would have worked very well and allowed you to have at least a partial position in a huge winner. Have a sell discipline; be willing to take partial profits.

◆ **Expectations.** It is wise to have an idea of what you are looking for when you enter a trade. Where do you expect the stock to go, what is the price objective, and where is the key resistance? Determining this before you enter a trade can then make it easier to sell out at least part of the position once that level is achieved.

◆ **Stop points.** There are times, despite all of your research and hard work, that a stock will go against you. The trade doesn't work out as planned. So just as you should have a sell discipline when things go your way, you must employ discipline if the trade doesn't work out. Identify your stop-loss point going into the trade, and then respect it. You want to avoid riding a stock down. For example, in 1999 Xerox (XRX) fell from a peak of 62 to less than 10. These types of disasters will ruin your year. Try to avoid them by adhering to your determined stop points. Remember to cut your losses short, and let your profits run.

◆ **Death row.** One way to perceive stops is that if a stock you own hits the stop-loss point, move it to death row. Then it becomes a question of when the stock gets executed! You can wait for a bounce back up to execute it—maybe a couple of days, giving the stock its last smoke. If the stock never bounces during this specified time frame, then shoot it.

If it does bounce, it is important to judge the quality of the bounce. Compare it to its peers. How is it acting, relatively speaking? Where is the first level of upside resistance? Was the stop point initially hit merely because the market in general sold off? These are the things to look at when trying to figure out whether the sentence of execution can be appealed or the stock should be killed immediately or even granted a pardon!

◆ **Bullish support line.** Watch for a violation of the long-term bullish support line. This is a negative for the stock and will often suggest that some type of defensive action be taken. This can often be a valid level for stopping out of a stock.

◆ **Review positions.** The only way you know if your stop-loss point has been hit, or if you are able to raise your stop-loss point, is by reviewing your positions on a regular basis. Make a daily habit of looking at the point and figure chart of each stock you own. The chart acts as your early warning system.

◆ **Hindsight.** Remember, hindsight is twenty-twenty. You must take the information available at the time and make a decision. Look at the weight of the evidence before you. Do not try to second-guess your instrument panel. You will not always be right. You may stop out of a stock, only to watch it go right back up. But if the technical picture has deteriorated sufficiently, be willing to take action. ❏

PLAY #64

Buy on Rumor, Sell on News:
Stick to the Reason You Bought the Stock

With respect to investing, we recommend that you write
down why you bought a specific stock. If the reasons you
bought a stock change, then you should sell the stock.
Or said another way, stick to the reason you bought a stock.

AS AN EXAMPLE, let's say you bought XYZ Corp. because you thought the stock was going to report great earnings. You bought 500 shares, anticipating that once the earnings report was announced, the stock would rise. That is your reason for buying the stock. In keeping with the above advice, once the earnings report is released and the stock reacts, you should sell it, whether it rallies sharply or plummets. Your reason for owning the stock no longer exists, now that the report has been released!

This tip goes hand in hand with the need to review your positions on a continual basis. By reviewing your holdings, you will be able to see if the reason(s) for buying a particular stock has changed. Then you can act accordingly, taking the appropriate action, whether it's selling or hedging the position.

So as we like to say, write down the reason you bought a stock, then stick to that reason. If the reason changes, take action. ❑

How Good Are Your Defensive Skills?

Think about your favorite football team for a second. If they played offense 100 percent of the time, they would be marginal at best. It is the same thing in the stock market. If you play offense 100 percent of the time, your returns are going to be marginal at best. Just as in football or any sport, there are times to play offense, and there are times to play defense. When you play defense, the opposing team is trying to score against you. Similarly, in the stock market the market "scores" against us by taking our hard-earned profits away.

MANY INVESTORS FALSELY assume that the only way to play defense is to sell their stocks. There are lots of different strategies to playing defense that are appropriate in different situations. For instance, a defense strategy for a thirty-year-old may not be as stringent as it would be for a sixty-five-year-old, who is going to require the use of his money much sooner. A defensive strategy for a trader could include short sales, whereas that may not be suitable for another investor.

Sharpening your defensive skills will improve your overall performance through a market cycle. As a general rule, the market goes up two-thirds of the time and down one-third. However, not playing some sort of defense during that downtime can severely hamper your overall performance, since stocks go down almost twice as fast as they go up! Below we have outlined some of the defensive plays we recommend once our bullish percent market indicators suggest defense.

◆ Come off margin.

◆ Don't initiate new positions, or at least initiate only partial positions.

◆ Instead of chasing stocks, wait for them to pull back to support levels on their charts to initiate positions.

◆ Pay close attention to sector rotation. Some sectors will top out ahead of the market, and some will bottom out before the rest of the market. If you must initiate new positions, do so in those sectors that are already oversold and showing signs of a bottom.

◆ If you do purchase stocks while the indicators are on defense, then make sure you have a stop loss selected when you make the transaction. If the stock then declines to the stop, execute your game plan and sell the stock. Don't let the emotion of the moment change a decision you made on an objective basis.

◆ For stocks that have rallied strongly, you may want to tighten up your stop loss or even take some profits. Notice that we said "some." This does not mean you have to sell all of your stock. If you own 500 shares of XYZ and have a nice profit in it, maybe you want to sell 200 or 250 or 300 shares. This will raise your cash position and get you ready for the next opportunity. We would rather lose opportunity than money, as there will always be another opportunity.

◆ If you have weak-performing stocks in your portfolios, this would be a good time to weed them out. If they were not performing when the market was doing OK, then they are not likely to do very well in a decline.

◆ Buy protective puts on the portfolio as insurance. Just as with home owners or car insurance, you hope you don't have to use it, but if there is a fire or an accident, you are sure glad you have that insurance. Your stock portfolio is the same way. You can also use index puts to hedge a whole account, too.

◆ Tighten up stop-loss points on existing positions. This leaves less capital at risk.

◆ Sell calls against a position or a portion of the position. This brings cash into the account as a hedge. With this strategy, you need to make sure you don't mind being called out of the stock. Realize that with this strategy the downside protection is limited. ❑

Hedging Your Portfolio with Index Options

A little insurance never hurt anyone.

MANY SO-CALLED market experts discount the use of options. However, if used correctly, options can be a very good way to transfer risk. One way to do this is via put options on your portfolio. If you have seen your portfolio do very well, but are now concerned about how a market decline would affect it, then the purchase of index puts might help you and at the same time ease some of that concern.

As most of you already know, puts give their owner the right, but not the obligation, to sell a stock or an index at a specified price within a given period of time. In the case of individual equities, you can sell the stock or sell the option. However, in the case of index options, you essentially sell the option and then receive the cash value based on your strike price and the closing value of the index. Index options give you a good way to protect or hedge the portfolio in the event of a market decline.

Let's digress a moment and take a look at why you would want to protect your portfolio from a market drop, using two mythical investors, Mr. Jones and Mr. Smith. Both had $100,000 and wanted to make 20 percent on an annual basis. If they achieved this goal, they figured they would have $120,000 after year one and $144,000 after year two. They had watched the market rally, but were beginning to wonder if it could continue. Mr. Smith then asked Mr. Jones what would happen if, instead of rising 20 percent, their portfolios fell by 20 percent. They once again did the math and figured their $100,000 account would fall to $80,000. It would then take a gain of 80 percent to reach their desired goal of $144,000 after year two.

Mr. Jones had an idea. He had learned about options and how they can be used to transfer risk. He remembered that puts could be used to protect gains or protect a portfolio. Should the market decline, then the puts would rise in value, offsetting potential losses in the portfolio. Should the market keep rising, he would lose only the premium he paid for the puts. After that, he would participate fully in any rally. Then, if the market declined and they had protected their portfolios, they would still have a reasonable chance to reach their goal of $144,000 at the end of the second year.

Once you decide you want to hedge your portfolio, then you must decide which index options to use. This is an important decision. If you have a blue-chip portfolio, one that moves closely with the S&P 100, then using the S&P 100 (OEX) puts would be appropriate. However, if your portfolio more closely resembles the Nasdaq 100 (NDX), then puts on this index would be better.

For our purposes, we will assume that our portfolio is oriented primarily toward blue chips and correlates closely with the S&P 100. Therefore, we will use OEX puts to show you how to arrive at the right number of puts to buy, although the prices we will use are fictitious. We will assume we have a portfolio valued at $1 million. Also, we will assume the OEX is trading around 800 with the put options due to expire nine months down the road, trading at $30. Each option would cost $3,000 ($30 x 100 = $3000).

To determine how many puts you need to purchase to hedge this portfolio, you simply divide the portfolio value by the dollar amount of the OEX. You can calculate the dollar amount as follows. The OEX is 800, and each put is multiplied by $100. In this case, we take $100 times 800 and arrive at $80,000 (800 x $100= $80,000). We then divide the portfolio value by $80,000 to arrive at the number of puts you need to buy. For this example, that would be 12.

We are showing an illustration in which the entire portfolio is being hedged. You may not want to hedge all of it. Perhaps you have a number of utility stocks, just as an example, and don't want to hedge those. Simply subtract the value of what you don't want to hedge and then do the division.

For our example, we are purchasing OEX puts with nine months until expiration. These are trading at $30, so that purchasing twelve of them would cost $36,000. In other words, buying these puts would bring the cost of this "insurance" to $36,000, or 3.6 percent of the portfolio value.

Now, what happens if the market declines? If the OEX falls 10 percent, the OEX would fall to approximately 720 and our 800 strike priced puts would rise to $80. This creates a profit of $60,000 and would offset the $100,000 loss in the portfolio. So with the puts as insurance, you would lose only about 4 percent, rather than the 10 percent the portfolio declined. While not hedging the entire amount, it certainly hedges the majority of it, and we feel it is very important to keep losses to a minimum. If the market fell 15 percent, the portfolio would decline to $850,000, a loss of $150,000. However, the OEX would fall to 680, and the puts would rise to $120, yielding a profit of $108,000. The net result is that you would lose about 4.2 percent rather than 15 percent, just a little more than the cost of the insurance.

If you have fears about the market, this strategy will give you a good way to keep any losses small in the event it does decline. ❑

PLAY # 6 7

No Free Lunch: Selling Calls against Your Not-For-Sale Stock

There is no free lunch.

ONE STRATEGY MANY investors use is the covered write, which is purchasing a stock and selling a call option against it. Selling the call obligates the investor to sell his stock at a given price, called the *strike price,* within a given period of time. This strategy is considered conservative enough to be allowed in IRA accounts. However, there is one way the covered write is not conservative, and that is by selling calls against stock that you have no intention of selling. This is what we call *closet uncovered writing.* Right now interest rates are at fairly low levels, and a number of investors are looking for ways to increase their income. The covered write is one strategy investors use for that purpose.

So, a closet uncovered writer is someone who is writing calls against a portfolio of stocks that he or she has no intention of selling for any number of reasons. For example, the writer might own low-cost stock, and selling it would present tax consequences. Or the stock may have been in the family for years, and the writer just can't bear to sell it. Or it may be a high-cost stock that someone doesn't want to sell at a loss.

Whatever the reason, when you sell covered calls against not-for-sale stock, you assume all of the risks of an uncovered writer. Should the stock on which you sold those calls rise beyond the option strike price, you must either

◆ roll the option up to a higher strike or out to a further month, most often at a net debit, or

◆ agree to assume the risk of a short position if exercised, or

◆ buy the stock to deliver if exercised.

By definition, a covered writer accepts option premium income and forgoes stock appreciation above the option strike price. The closet uncovered writer is looking for a free lunch. He thoroughly enjoys the premium income, but never intends to give up his stock. This strategy can be hazardous to your portfolio's health. Few investors are disciplined enough or well-capitalized enough to assume the risk of uncovered call writing.

When you begin a covered writing program, either set aside capital to purchase new stock on which to sell calls, or sell calls only on the stocks you hold that you are willing to sell at a particular price. Remember, there is *no* free lunch. ❑

PLAY #68

Augmented Writing

Don't be afraid to sell higher.

VERY OFTEN WE HEAR investors say they wish they could sell one of their stocks at a higher price. This is often after the stock they would like to sell has already rallied. It's not that they are greedy, just that everyone would like to sell at a higher price. There is an option strategy that could help you accomplish this goal, one that works best when you have 1,000 or more shares. Let's take a look at this strategy, which we call *augmented writing*.

Augmented writing involves selling calls against your position in the hope that down the road you will sell that stock at a higher price. Because you are selling calls, augmented writing allows you to take in premium today, while waiting for the stock to reach a targeted sales price. The interesting thing with augmented writing is that we don't sell calls against the entire position to begin with. We only sell calls against a portion of the position. Should the stock rally, we buy back those calls and then sell enough calls at a higher price to offset that purchase. We continue this pattern until we have sold calls with a strike price at or above the price we would like to sell. If the options expire worthless along the way, then we can begin the strategy anew or sell more calls with the same strike price with a later expiration.

Here is an example of the strategy. We will assume that XYZ stock is trading around 57 and that you hold 2,000 shares. You would like to sell the stock at 75, but that is 18 points above its current price and would require a 30 percent gain in the stock. So, what do we do? The first thing we would do is to sell five May 60 calls (or calls whose expiration are four to six months from when you sell) at 2⅞ against your position. Should the third Friday in May come and XYZ is trading below 60, then the calls expire worthless and you can rewrite against your position. However, if XYZ is trading above 60, whether at expiration or before, you can then buy back those May 60 calls and sell ten August 65 calls, or sell calls whose expiration is three months further out. The selling of the August calls should cover the cost of buying back the May 60 calls. You can then repeat this process all the way up to 75 by continually writing approximately twice as many options as you buy back until you are fully written. The point is that you use the proceeds from the sale of the additional calls to pay for the buyback and you don't have to put up more money. Extra money is never put up, but flows in whenever any options expire and are rewritten.

We want to mention one caveat here, though: You must be willing to sell the stock. If you are not willing to sell, then the best bet is not even to begin this strategy. If you are interested in selling, especially at a higher price, then the augmented writing strategy is one to consider. ❑

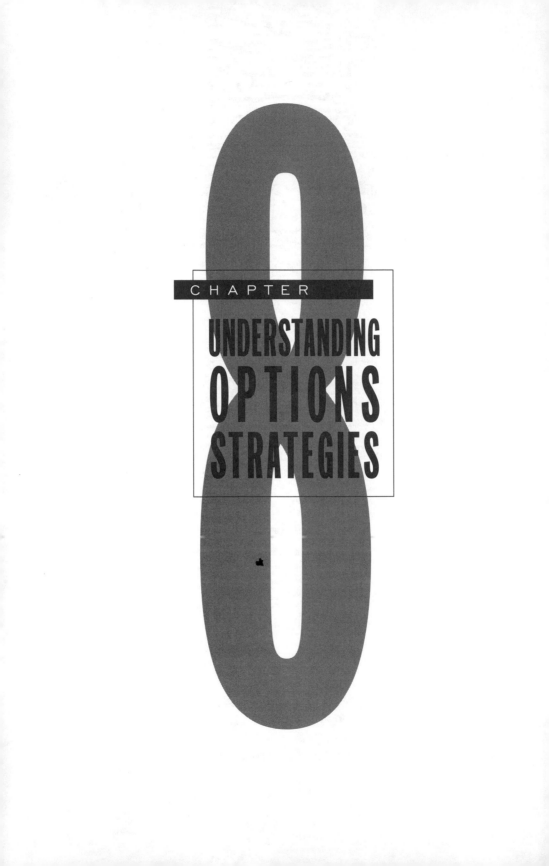

CHAPTER

UNDERSTANDING OPTIONS STRATEGIES

EVERY SUNDAY before the game starts, the training room is filled. Football players are getting ankles taped, knees wrapped, and equipment adjusted, all to prevent the risk of injury. Just as the equipment manager and athletic trainer are an integral part of the overall health of a football team, understanding the benefit of options strategies can potentially improve the health of your portfolio. An ill-conceived options strategy can result in portfolio injury. Expertise and good judgment is required for those who choose to use options. The following tips will bring you closer to understanding the intricacies of options and how to effectively use them as a risk management tool.

The Key to Understanding Options

Understanding option strategies can
be as easy as simple arithmetic.

IN THE MID-1970s I decided to become an expert in options. Back then there were no easy-to-understand books on the subject, nor were there any classes being taught. The only way to learn the subject was to go home with a legal pad and paper and work out all of the different option strategies by hand. Remember working over math problems in college, over and over and over again, until you had committed them to memory? That's the way I learned the options business.

Along the way, it occurred to me that the key to understanding all option strategies was simply understanding the definitions of a put and a call. In other words, at expiration, when there is no time premium left to consider, all option strategies boil down to simple arithmetic. On expiration day there are no gray areas. An option either has value or it does not have value. In the case of a call, if the stock is above the exercise price, the call has value. Conversely, if the stock is below the exercise price, the call has no value. The same works for a put in reverse.

Each piece of a multilateral option strategy can be evaluated separately and then netted out. Ask yourself the question, "What did I pay and eventually what did I get?" and you'll realize that it's simple arithmetic. There still isn't any easy way to learn options other than to get a cup of coffee and begin to evaluate, at expiration, hypothetical positions. All you have to do is to write down where you think the stock will be at expiration and then evaluate each piece of the strategy separately. Since there are no gray areas in options at expiration, it becomes a very elementary exercise. Try it. You will be surprised at how fast this seemingly complex investment vehicle becomes as simple as pie. ❑

Definition of a Call and Put

Options are a viable tool to use as an investment vehicle. But before you embark on any type of option strategy, you should understand the basic definition of a call and put. Only then can you decide if options have a place in your portfolio.

AS THE NAME IMPLIES, an option is a choice. In financial terms, an option is the right to buy or sell specific securities at a specified price within a specified time. There are two types of stock options—calls and puts.

A *call* gives you the right to buy 100 shares of the underlying stock at a specific price for a predetermined time period. As an example, if you bought a three-month call option on XYZ stock at $40, you would own the right to buy XYZ at $40 per share (specific price) anytime over the next three months (the predetermined time period). The buyer of the call pays a *premium* to the seller of the call. Given this, you would buy a call option if you expected the stock to rise in price.

A *put* gives you the right to sell 100 shares of the underlying stock at a particular price for a specific time period. Because of this, when the underlying stock drops in price, the put owner can buy the stock in the open market at the current price (which is now lower), then immediately sell the stock at a higher price (the predetermined *exercise* or *strike price* from when the put option was

BULLISH (EXPECT STOCK'S PRICE TO RISE)	BEARISH (EXPECT STOCK'S PRICE TO DROP)
Buy Call	Buy Put
Sell Put	Sell Call

purchased), thereby making a profit. The buyer of the put pays a premium to the seller of the put. In summary, you would buy a put option if you expected the stock to fall in price.

If you sell the call or put, you are considered the *writer* of that option. The writer is paid the premium for giving up his right. The call or put buyer pays this to the writer. ❑

The Options Delta:
An Important Term to Know

You don't have to understand Greek to realize the importance of this options term. You only get that point-for-point move when deep in the money.

THERE ARE PLENTY of terms from the Greek alphabet used in the options business that can easily confuse an investor. Terms like *delta, gamma, theta,* and *omega* are all associated with options trading, but if you are an individual investor, there is only one you need to know. It's the option's *delta.* When I first began trading options in the mid-1970s, I thought all options moved point-for-point with the underlying stock. We all looked at options as simply cheap stocks back then.

The market had just gone through the worst bear market since the 1929 crash, and most investors lost 50 percent to 70 percent of their equity. The listed options business started in April 1973 and was still very new when I started in the business in 1974. Investors gravitated to this new product because the cost of call options was far less than putting up the money to buy the actual shares of the underlying stocks themselves. We as brokers didn't know much about this new product, either.

Had I learned a little about delta, I might have been able to help my clients make money in this new game rather than to fail them miserably, on balance. It wasn't until later that I learned that options don't move point-for-point with the underlying stock until they move deep in the money.

What do I mean by *deep in the money*? Let's say a stock is trading at $50 per share. If you buy a call option with an exercise price at $50, where the stock is now trading, we call that an at-the-money call. If you buy a call option with an exercise price five points above the current market price of the stock, or in this case $55, we call that an out-of-the money call. Conversely, if you buy a call with an exercise price below the current market price of the underlying stock, or in this case an exercise price of $45, we call that an in-the-money call.

Here is a rule of thumb that has worked for me. An at-the-money call has a delta in the area of 0.50. This means that for each point move in the underlying stock, the call options in this example will move one-half point. For the option that is five points out of the money, in this case the 55 call, the option will move about one-quarter point for each point in the underlying stock. For the option that is five points in the money, in this case the 45 call, the delta, or point move in the option for each point move in the underlying stock, will approximate three-quarters of a point. This is a rule of thumb and only a rule of thumb. There are computer programs that will give you much more exact numbers. But it is important to understand that options don't move point-for-point with the underlying stock until they move deep in the money. In the example above, we might find that a call option with an exercise price of $35, with the stock currently trading at $50, might approximate a point-for-point move with the underlying stock. ❏

PLAY # 7 2

Call Guidelines

By following some basic guidelines, call options
can be an effective risk management tool.

CALL OPTIONS OFFER A low-risk as well as a limited way to play an individual stock, without putting up a great deal of money. Keeping this in mind, here are some guidelines for you to consider when you purchase call options. Calls give the investor the right to buy a specific stock at a specific price (the strike price) within a given period of time (expiration). Calls are typically purchased to play an upside move in a stock or an index. Now, on to the guidelines:

◆ **First, no matter how well devised or thought out your option strategy is, you will not be profitable unless your opinion of the underlying stock is correct.** Consequently, before you even consider which options to buy, take a close look at the technical picture of the stock. Remember, this will tell you when to buy a stock. You also want to make sure the stock is trending up and is outperforming the market. Charting your own stocks will let you know which stocks are breaking out and which are breaking down.

◆ **Second, diversify!** While you may be quite bullish on the auto stocks, buying calls on General Motors, Ford, and Daimler-Chrysler would be a mistake. Buying options involves some risk, so spread that risk around. Don't put all of your eggs in one basket. Buy options in different industry groups and with different expiration months.

◆ **Third, buy in-the-money (ITM) calls.** Choosing an out-of-the-money (OTM) option may leave you right on the stock, but with a loss in your option if the stock doesn't rise enough. Successful investors not only anticipate what can go right, but also what can go wrong. An in-the-money option will help you to preserve your capital. The saying "you get what you pay for" applies to options, too. Out-of-the-money options may be cheap, but that is only because they generally aren't worth much. In our daily report, all of our call and put recommendations are in the money. The reason we suggest you use in-the-money calls is that options do not move point-for-point with the stock until it is very deep in the money.

The term we use to express this relationship, as mentioned before, is *delta*. The delta will tell you how much the option will move in relation to the stock. Typically, ITM options have higher deltas while OTM options have lower deltas. For example, a call option on a stock with a delta of 0.50 means that for each one-point move in the stock, the call option will move one-half point, whether up or down. As the stock moves higher, the delta will move up. A stock decline will move the delta lower.

From this very brief discussion of the deltas, it is probably already apparent to you that you can buy an out-of-the-money call on a stock, have the stock rise and still lose money. In other words, you would be dead right on the direction of the stock, but would still lose money.

◆ **Fourth, buy time.** Always choose an option with at least three to four months left in its life. Any strategy should be given time to work. Options with less time can only make things more difficult, including your decisions. Very often, buying enough time will give you a chance to get out of your calls if they have initially gone against you.

◆ **Fifth, buy only as many options as you would round lots of stock.** If you typically buy 500 shares of stock, then buy five calls. Do not overleverage yourself by purchasing more than five calls. This can be a dangerous situation if you allow it to happen. ❑

PLAY # 73

More Call Guidelines

Take it from experience: You need to do your homework on the underlying stock.

HERE'S A STRATEGY that has been used, twisted, and distorted. It's gotten a bad rap in the investment community simply because it is the strategy that is most often abused. Read the discussion of overleveraging on pages 178–179 and you will see what I mean. In the 1970s, when these investment products were first listed, there were only about twenty-nine stocks with calls attached to them, and even fewer with puts. We really didn't know much about them other than that they were cheap. They caught on quickly because they offered tremendous leverage. One could control thousands of dollars of stock for a very small investment. This had mass appeal. It's the same old "get rich quick" scheme, and some investors really did.

I'll never forget my very first options play. It was on Flying Tiger Cargo Airlines February 15 calls. Flying Tiger, symbol TGR, was one of those volatile issues and was one of the few that had options attached to it. It was a natural. The Flying Tiger BCs, or February 15 calls, were going for $1.50, and the stock was trading at $13. I can remember this as vividly as if it were yesterday. At the time, I was making $9,000 a year and thought I was in tall clover. Trading options offered a way to increase my salary with very little effort. I made my bet. I bought ten contracts of the Flying Tiger BCs. That cost me $1,500, plus commissions. This was in January.

I had six weeks until these options expired. It was kind of like six weeks to watch the fruit on a slot machine roll around until it comes to rest. I was dead right on the stock. It began to rise slowly. Heck, I was only asking the stock to rise two points in six weeks so that the call option I had bought would expire worthless. That's only 15.3 percent during that period, or about 135 percent on an annualized basis. Sounded reasonable to me. No problem here. For me to make any money past commissions I only needed the stock to rise to $17.50 or 34.6 percent, which is annualized 308 percent. That's for me to have enough for lunch after commissions. For me to make a real hit, well, why calculate it—you get the picture.

Here's what happened. The stock rose in price to $13.75, $14, $14.25, and $14.75, and my call option was going down $1.50, $1.13, $1, $0.75, $0.63, $0.38, and so on to eventual evaporation. The stock ended up at about $15. The stock rose as I expected, but I lost my ever-loving rear end. Not only that, but I couldn't afford to lose 16 percent of my salary in one trade. This is why I'll never forget this trade as long as I live.

What's wrong with this picture? First, I did not do enough homework on the underlying stock. I didn't know how to do any homework on the underlying stock back then (even if I wanted to). I simply read the company research report, which had a 1-1 on it, meaning it was OK to buy for the short term, and OK to buy for the long term. The research report did not say anything about wild option plays on the stock. If I had had the education, I would have made sure the stock was above the trend line, with positive relative strength and the RS chart in a column of Xs. It should have just pulled back to within 10 percent of the trend line, allowing me to buy on a pullback, or on sale, if you will.

Next, I overleveraged. I bought more calls than I would have normally had money to buy round lots of the stock. In fact, I bought about nine more calls than I had money to buy the stock, had I chosen that route. I could have bought about 100 shares of the stock with the money I had. This suggests that I should have bought only one call. Instead, I bought ten calls with that same $1,500 and in essence traded myself up to a 1,000-share buyer.

Finally, I bought a call expiring in six weeks. Six weeks is the line of demarcation at which option premiums begin to evaporate most rapidly. Time is an important piece of the equation when pricing options. The closer to expiration you get, the faster the premium evaporates. I should have bought time. Instead, I bought an out-of-the-money call. The stock had to rise two points just for me to lose everything. I should have paid more and bought an in-the-money-call, which would have had almost a point-for-point move with the stock.

You see, this is not as easy a game to play as most investors think. There are many moving parts that must be taken into consideration. Do your homework or don't use this product! ❏

PLAY #74

Put Guidelines

Don't buy blindly. Have some rules to help you
initiate positions, whether in options or stocks.

ONE OF THE FAVORITE strategies for investors wanting to play a decline in a stock is the use of put options. Puts give the investor the right to sell a specific stock at a specific price (the strike price) within a given period of time (expiration). If the investor believes a particular stock is headed lower, then he can simply purchase a put. He does not have to wait for an uptick in the option, as he would if he were to sell the particular stock short. We typically like to purchase puts when our market indicators dictate that there is risk in the market. This would occur when the NYSE Bullish Percent is at high levels and reverses to the downside or when our short-term indicators give sell signals.

We would like to give you some guidelines for the purchase of puts. Of course, if you buy puts on a stock that is skyrocketing, then you are not going to be successful—regardless. However, these guidelines will give you a better chance of being successful and having a profitable trade if, in fact, your stocks head down. So here are those guidelines:

1 Always buy in-the-money puts. Unlike calls, puts hold much of their time premium when out of the money, but lose it fast when in the money.

2 Buy time. Even if you plan to be invested for only a week, the middle option will hold up better than the near option in a sideways market or one that trades in a range. It will also give you a second chance in many cases if the stock rallies first and then heads down. If you purchase the near option and see the stock rally, by the time the stock comes back down, that option will be ready to expire or will already have expired.

3 Diversify. Do not put all of your eggs (or puts) in one basket. You can diversify by industry group and expiration month. Although you may be bearish on Delta Airlines, AMR Corp., and UAL Inc., you don't have to buy puts on all three.

4 Take action if your stock opinion changes! Do not forget why you initiated the trade in the first place. This goes for the indicators, too. Should they turn positive, you may want to head for the sidelines with your put positions.

5 Don't buy more puts than you would sell short the stock. If you would short 500 shares of a stock, then buy only five puts. Don't overleverage the position. This is a sure way to get into trouble. Remember, you can lose 100 percent in a put position, and that is not likely to occur with a stock. ❑

PLAY #75

More Put Guidelines

The stock selection is paramount to
the success of the put-buying strategy.

MOST OF US THINK OF puts as a substitute for selling short. This is often the case and does provide a much less risky way of making a bet on a stock's decline. The first thing an investor must consider when buying a put is exactly what he thinks the underlying stock will do. The stock is paramount to the success of the put buying strategy. If he's wrong on the stock, he'll be wrong on the put.

What are the attributes a stock should have before it qualifies for a put purchase? First, the stock should have fundamental problems. One possible way of determining this is to keep track of *Value Line*'s ranking system. A stock that is declining in rank probably has a problem with its fundamentals, as seen by *Value Line*. Standard & Poor's has a great service, too, and one can keep track of that ranking system. Possibly you do your own fundamental work. Whatever you do, the fundamentals should be less than optimum.

Next, the stock should be trading below its long-term trend line. This suggests the stock is already in a downtrend. Within the confines of a downtrend, we like the stock to have just bounced back to within 10 percent of that trend line.

Relative strength is very important in this evaluation. Preferably the relative strength should be negative versus the Dow Jones or S&P 500, and the relative strength point and figure chart should be in a column of Os, signifying that it is currently underperforming the market. When you calculate its normal distribution or ten-week trading band, it should be on the overbought side of the curve for optimum results. This takes into consideration only the underlying stock.

Now let's look at what option to select. We discussed the term *delta*. We prefer to buy in-the-money puts, since they have a much higher correlation to a one-point move in the underlying stock versus an out-of-the-money put. The option should carry a fair to undervalued valuation. This helps ensure you are not paying too much. (The Chicago Board Options Exchange [CBOE] has an options valuation calculator at www.cboe.com.)

Be sure to buy at least three-month puts or longer so you give the strategy enough time to work out. We even like to hold the option to expiration, which ensures we take the trading aspect out of the strategy. This is discussed a little later in this chapter.

Sounds like a lot of calculations, doesn't it? Who ever said investing was easy? The whole idea with this formula is to try to stack as many odds in your favor as possible when you embark on a trade. ❑

Overleveraging an Options Position

Options should not be viewed merely as inexpensive stocks.
Investors who do not follow this tenet often set
themselves up for failure as a result of overleveraging.

IT TOOK ME A LONG TIME and many failed trades to understand what overleveraging was. When I was a stockbroker in the
mid-1970s, the listed options business was in its infancy, and I had
learned just enough about it to be dangerous. We simply looked at
options as inexpensive stocks. We had no idea they had the potential to be time bombs.

Having just experienced the worst bear market since the crash of
1929, investors weren't too interested in venturing back into the
world of equities. Options were of interest, however, because of
their low price. Investors wanted to make money in the stock market, but were gun-shy about making a full commitment to equities
again. The average investor's only experience in the markets, for
the most part, was in purchasing equities and paying the full price,
either on a cash basis or on margin. Options were so inexpensive
relative to the full cost of the underlying stock that it was very easy
to overleverage a position when purchasing them.

Mr. Jones was, let's say, a 200-share buyer of stock priced in the
$20 range, meaning that he generally paid about $4,000 for a stock
purchase. Through independent study, he learned about the
mechanics of trading options. What he found most appealing
about the options business was the limited risk factor and that the
option to buy the same underlying stock he would normally have
purchased was trading at only a fraction of the actual cost of the
stock. Let's say he priced an at-the-money call option on XYZ stock
and found that a six-month call was selling for $5. Since each call
option represents 100 shares of stock, one call was valued at $5 x
100 shares=$500. That was a far cry from the normal cost of buying
100 shares of stock at $20 per share. In Mr. Jones' mind this rep-
resented a savings of $1,500, and if he were correct in his assump-

tion, the stock would rise. The option would participate in that advance. So Mr. Jones figured that if he normally spent $4,000 for the purchase of stock in the past, he could afford to buy eight contracts of XYZ six-month, at-the-money calls, priced at $5 per share.

What did Mr. Jones just do? He spent the same amount of money he normally spent when purchasing stock. Here's where the trouble starts. He normally was a 200-share buyer. That 200-share purchase is the equivalent of two call options. He just bought eight call options with the $4,000, and in effect leveraged himself up to an 800-share buyer. If, at expiration, the stock was below the exercise price, those calls would expire worthless, and Mr. Jones would have just lost his entire investment.

The key to not overleveraging an investment in options is to buy only as many calls or puts as you would normally have an appetite for in 100-share round lots of the underlying stock. This way investing in options can become very fruitful. ❑

PLAY # 77

When Investing in Options, Buy Time

Time is the silent killer of all options. One of the main ingredients in options pricing is time left to expiration.

WHEN YOU HAVE DONE your homework on the underlying stock and have determined you will have better leverage investing in the options, buy time. There is a rule of thumb that when an option moves into the "six-week-to-expiration" envelope, the time premium begins to melt like an ice cream cone on Coney Island in July. When you enter that six-week envelope, consider rolling that contract out to the next expiration date. Trading options is difficult enough without letting Father Time undermine your plans.

Here is the dirty little secret to making money in the markets. Making money in the market takes time. It is not an overnight phenomenon. In many cases the underlying stock of the option you purchased will do virtually nothing over a three-month period. Think back to Statistics 101. When you evaluate a bell curve or the normal distribution, you will find that whatever you are studying will remain within one standard deviation 68 percent of the time. In the option business, a move of one standard deviation will not be enough to overcome premium over intrinsic value and the commissions in and out. You will need a move higher than that. What this means is that you need to give the stock time to do what you expect it to do.

I so often see option traders buying one-month calls and then wonder why their premium melted away. I would buy at least six months' time to expiration and then—listen to this—then, hold the contract until expiration. This does two things: It takes the trading aspect out of options, and it gives the stock time to move enough to give you a potentially rewarding return for the risk you are taking.

I can tell you this: if I had held every option I ever bought until expiration, I would be far better off. I remember one recommendation I made on CNBC. I'll never forget this. Susie Gharib, in the last second of the show, said, "Tom, what is your number-one stock pick?" The question came from out of the blue, and I had to say something. Lucent came to mind as a stock we were recently recommending. The stock was around $40, if I remember correctly, and she said, "Boy, the stock is already up from the telephone spinoff from $27." I said, "No problem."

When I got back to my office that afternoon I decided to put my money where my mouth was. I bought something like 1,000 shares of Lucent that day. It subsequently went to $144, split two for one and then rose back to the $100 area. What a hit! I held it through the whole run.

Now think for a second what most option traders would have done. More than likely, an option trader would have bought a three-month $40 call for, let's say, $4 per share times 100 shares a contract, or $400. The option then would have risen to $8, or $800, in short order. Most option traders would have taken the profit, thinking how smart they were to make a 100 percent return on their investment. Had they bought a six-month call they could have ridden on their investment from $400 to $6,000 per contract, and that is before the two for one split and the subsequent run-up back to $100 post-split. Now we're talking real money. All it takes is one play like that a year and you're home free. Buy time, and have patience. ❑

An Option Trader's Lesson from the Gym

Use options expiration to your advantage.
Sometimes holding until then can make the difference
between a good trade and a great trade.

ONE OF THE PEOPLE I have met at Wolfgang's Gym is an options trader. He and his wife have begun seriously trading options, and are doing well, I might add. About seven months ago he came to me to discuss my philosophy on options trading. I told him that one of the major benefits to buying options is that they give you staying power when the underlying stock moves in the wrong direction. If you are long the stock, there is a point at which the pain becomes too great on your portfolio, and you will have to throw in the towel and stop out. You can't be long 500 shares of VA Linux Systems (LNUX), once as high as $244 and now at $7. There is a point at which you either stop out of the stock or get wiped out. Owning the call option in either of these two stocks gives you staying power to hold on until expiration. They could come back as fast as they went down. For instance, Checkpoint (CHKP) was at $150 in October 2000, fell to $95, and is now back at $150.

Here is the point: I suggested to this person that in each of the calls he owned at that time, he hold them until expiration. If he had done his homework on the underlying stock, he should give it as much time to work as possible. Since he already knew the total amount he was risking, he should hold on until expiration. He wondered whether he would be better off trading them, since these stocks moved so fast. As our conversation continued, I suggested to him that he write down the prices of all his positions and revisit them once again on expiration date. Then he would let me know how he did.

Yesterday at the gym, the investor came up to me and said, "Tom, remember when you told me to keep track of my positions and get back with you on expiration day?" I said I did, and asked how well he had done. He said he made $6,000 trading the options we had discussed six months earlier. He then said that had he held them to expiration in September, he would have made $60,000.

The problem with this philosophy is that it goes totally against human nature. Investors feel the options market is here only for wild trading and nothing else. However, all it takes is one out of five to really fly, and you have a successful program going. In the life of one call option, one could have ridden Ciena (CIEN) from $30 to $100. Put the pencil to that and you start seeing real money. Think about it the next time you buy a package of calls. ❏

PLAY #79

Puts as Insurance

Puts can protect your portfolio in the event of an accident, just as your car or home insurance does.

THE BEST WAY TO THINK of a put option is as an insurance product. One of the questions I often ask a group of people I am speaking to is "How many of you out there own a put option?" The crowd looks bewildered and very few, if any, raise their hand. I then come back with the question, "How many of you own an automobile?" Everyone raises a hand. I then make the statement, "If you own a car, you own a put." This is the case, because everyone who owns an automobile has purchased insurance on it. The contract you have with the insurance company basically states that if you have an accident in your car you have the right to put, or sell, that car to the insurance company for a certain amount of money, during a certain amount of time, and you must pay a premium to the insurance company to take that risk and issue you a policy.

The put option is exactly the same. The owner of the put has the right to sell stock to a person (Options Clearing Corporation*) for a certain price during the life of the contract, and he must pay a premium to the seller to purchase that put agreement. It's simply an insurance policy on your stock, should your stock experience an accident. So, when an investor buys 100 shares of stock and simultaneously buys a put option, he is in effect insuring his stock position.

The seller of the put is on the other side of the contract, the one who is perfectly willing and able to take the risk of buying that stock at the stipulated price (exercise price) and stands ready to do so for the life of the contract. For taking this risk, he is paid a premium by the put buyer. So we have two parties to the put contract, the investor, who is unwilling to take the risk of owning the underlying stock and thus transfers that risk to the put seller or "underwriter," who is willing to take the risk. The put buyer pays the premium that the put seller collects.

Okay, let's take an example. I buy XYZ stock for $40 and simultaneously buy a January 40 put for $4, or $400 per contract. If XYZ declines to $0, what is my risk? Let's think about this for a second. I bought the right to sell this stock to the underwriter discussed above, at the price of $40. For that privilege I paid $4, or $400 per contract of 100 shares. So if the stock goes to $0, my risk is only the cost of the insurance, or $400.

Let's look at another strategy that carries the same risk. You could instead choose to buy a January 40 call, let's say, at $4, or $400 per contract. This time I did not put up the money to buy the stock for $4,000. You are now thinking, "I wouldn't buy calls, that's too speculative. Since I am very conservative, buying stock and buying the put for insurance is less risky and more in line with my risk tolerances."

Now for the magic. If the stock declines to $0, what is my risk? Well, I paid $4, or $400 for the call, and the stock went down, so my call is now worthless. I lost $400. What did you lose in buying the stock and buying the put as insurance? You lost the cost of the insurance when the stock went to $0, which was $400. What if the stock went to $100? Your profit in the long stock-long put would be $40 - $100 - $4 for the put, or 56 points.

What about the long call? It would be the $40 strike price minus $100 at expiration, minus the cost of the $4 call, or 56 points. It appears the risks are exactly the same. Buying calls and buying stock and simultaneously buying a put as insurance are equivalent strategies.

How did I figure this out? Just think about what the option strategy is trying to accomplish. Then determine if there is another option strategy that accomplishes the same thing. This is called option equivalents. In another discussion on options, we analyze the uncovered put. Did you know this was an equivalent strategy to the covered write? Interesting, isn't it?

*NOTE: The Options Clearing Corporation is the registered clearing agency of all options listed on stock exchanges in the United States and is subject to regulation by the Securities and Exchange Commission. ❏

PLAY #80

Uncovered Puts:
Be Sure You Can Pay for Them

It's not just a case of collecting premiums and never having to pay out in liabilities. You must understand the risk before selling the yellows.

OVER THE YEARS I have seen the uncovered put strategy abused and misunderstood more than any other strategy in the options business. The justification for the existence of the listed options markets is that it allows the transfer of risk. The put option business is similar to the insurance business. Selling put options is similar to the business of underwriting. A person who practices the business of insuring anything is called an underwriter because he writes his name at the foot of the insurance policy. An insurance underwriter simply accepts a premium in return for accepting a risk. The success of this operation depends on the amount of premium he takes in and his ability to evaluate the associated risk he is assuming, very much like the situation with health or automobile insurance. The writer or seller of the put accepts the risk of the underlying stock declining in price. His risk, said another way, is the cost of ownership of the underlying stock at some predetermined price. Just as in the insurance business, the success of the put seller depends on the amount of premium he takes in and his ability to evaluate the risks associated with the stock he is contracting to buy.

The buyer of puts can be viewed as the insurance buyer. When the risk is too great in any particular endeavor, one seeks to reduce that risk by buying insurance. The long put functions like an insurance policy should the underlying stock have an accident and decline in price. The reason is the purchaser of a put has the right to "put," or sell stock, at a given price at a certain time in the future. For that right, he pays a certain consideration to the underwriter, as discussed above.

Another term for risk is *volatility* in the short term. Longer-term fundamental analysis becomes increasingly important. However, most put sales do not extend much past what one would call short term.

Because so many professional organizations are attempting to find the fair market value of put options, premium evaluation will prove profitable only to the largest and most efficient operations. Therefore, the majority of put writers should assume that the option market is efficient. We feel that the put writer will be better rewarded for time spent in technical analysis, since most option expirations are somewhat short term.

The equivalent of selling or underwriting puts is covered writing. The reason is that both strategies offer limited upside potential past the premium taken in and leaves substantial downside risk past the protection of the premium taken in.

Here's where the problem starts. When the market has risen, as it has since 1982, investors begin to think that stocks just can't go down. If stocks never had accidents, the best business to be in when investing would be the insurance business. The writer of puts would simply collect premiums and never have to pay out in liabilities.

The options exchanges have exacted margin requirements to carry an uncovered put position. Keep in mind that this requirement is simply a good-faith deposit of sorts to insure the writer of the put has the money to fulfill the contract, should he be called on to do so. This margin can be put up through fully paid securities, T-Bills, or anything else that is marginable. This margin requirement is less than the normal margin to buy securities, which is set at 50 percent. Because it is really only a good-faith deposit, investors have a tendency to sell more puts than they really have cash available with which to fulfill the contracts, if required to do so. In a major, unexpected market decline, such as we had in October 1987 and April 2000, the losses can be devastating.

Always be sure you carry in available cash or margin 50 percent of the exercise price of that contract you are underwriting, just in case you experience an unexpected market crash. Remember, only contract to purchase stock in the amount of 100-share round lots that you have an appetite and purse to own.

A friend of mine who worked back in the old put-and-call days, before listed options, told me about some advice he got from his boss. Back then the call tickets were green and the put tickets were yellow. His boss told him, "Bill, never sell the yellows; they always come back to you." ❑

PLAY # 8 1

Buy, Sell, Hold, or Hedge?

Using statistics in stock evaluation suggests that most
of the time a stock is considered a "hold." With this in mind,
one option strategy to employ is renting out your stock.
By this I mean selling covered calls.

WHETHER TO BUY, SELL, or hold is the underlying theme of this trading tip. It has to do with the normal distribution. Remember that concept in Statistics 101? The whole concept of winning in the stock market is to buy low and sell high, but what about that hold recommendation? All too often, the hold recommendation is nothing more than an analyst saying, "I have no idea what to do." Interestingly enough, 68 percent of the time stocks are languishing around that no-man's-land.

Louis Bachelier, in his 1900 doctoral thesis at the Sorbonne University in Paris, determined that stock prices were normally distributed. His thesis was called "The Theory of Speculation." He concluded that while the market was in flux, one could not apply statistical analysis to it. One must stop the motion of the market and then apply statistical analysis. In so doing, one could determine its next logical movement. In essence, he was suggest-

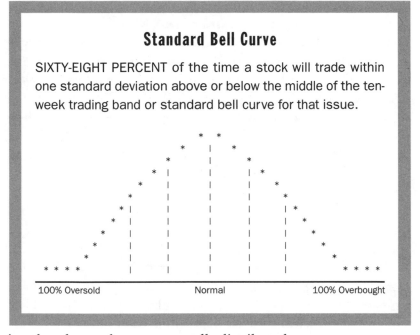

Standard Bell Curve

SIXTY-EIGHT PERCENT of the time a stock will trade within one standard deviation above or below the middle of the ten-week trading band or standard bell curve for that issue.

| 100% Oversold | Normal | 100% Overbought |

ing that the market was normally distributed.

Remember the old bell curve? That's what it's all about. The concept suggests that stock prices are destined to spend the majority of time in an area that is neither significantly high or low. This is why options premiums are small in relation to the full price of the underlying stock. Although the full range of the price of the stock might be large, most of those observations are expected to be around the mean of those prices.

In the past, before the advent of listed options, stocks in this no-man's-land would be rated a hold. This area of the bell curve encompasses one standard deviation above or below trend (**STANDARD BELL CURVE**).

Statistically speaking, this area of the bell curve happens 68 percent of the time. After the advent of listed options, this hold recommendation has changed to "hedge." In other words, if stocks tend to do nothing 68 percent of the time, then it would stand to reason that one could profit from renting one's stocks out 68 percent of the time. When I say rent out one's stock, I am referring to selling covered calls. Simply stated, since the markets are normally distributed, covered writing is applicable the majority of time.

Consider a stock trading near its mean price on the bell curve. This would be near dead center and carry a fifty-fifty probability of rising or falling. Most analysts would probably have a hold on the stock; however, with options, an investor can change the risk/reward or probability of success in the trade by selling a call option against the position. By selling the call option, the investor is effectively reducing the cost of the underlying stock and in essence shifting the stock further down the oversold side of the bell curve. The offset for such a strategy is that the profit potential is also diminished.

When the market or sector is skewed to the left side of the bell curve, the strategy that makes the most sense is simply long stock or long calls. Conversely, when the market or sector is skewed to the right side of the bell curve, the appropriate strategy is protecting profits, selling short, or buying puts. I find it useful when using point and figure analysis to keep the relative position of the bell curve on whatever I'm evaluating firmly in my mind.

A great friend of mine, the late Jim Yates, brought this concept to new heights. He created an "Options Strategy Spectrum," which was similar to a bell curve. The spectrum had six zones, or standard deviations, and it suggested different strategies for different areas of the bell curve. His accuracy in predicting market movement was second to none. ❑

PLAY #82

Selecting the Right Covered Write

All too often, investors will select a covered write
because it carries a very high option premium, and thus
a high called and static return. I know: I was one of
those investors, or, should I say, stockbrokers.

I ROUTINELY SELECTED covered writing candidates on the basis of their returns and virtually nothing else. This method of selection leaves much to be desired. First, any strategy that requires you to buy stock dictates that you begin by diligently researching the underlying stock. Your money is going into the purchase of the stock, so it should be a stock you want to own and that you feel will rise in price. Otherwise, there is no reason under the sun to buy the stock.

Here's why selection by annual returns often leads to disaster. The most important ingredient of option premium is volatility. The higher the volatility, the higher the option premium. When this high premium is factored into a static and called return on the covered write strategy, it looks very enticing indeed. The problem is that the premium is high for a reason—the underlying stock is extremely volatile. It has a high probability of moving significantly lower or higher. If you have not been diligent on both fundamentals and technicals, you might be buying a stock that is in a downtrend, has bad fundamentals, and has high volatility. These ingredients make for a strategy that can create severe losses to an account.

It is imperative that you do the research on the underlying stock first, both fundamental and technical. Then consider that if you write a call on that stock you will cap off your upside potential and at the same time leave most of the downside risk intact. Look at it this way: a diversified portfolio of stocks is designed to spread the risk. Some stocks in the portfolio will do very well, some will not do much, and some will decline in price. When evaluated in the aggregate, the portfolio should outperform the broad averages.

In a covered write, you effectively cap off the good stocks and leave most of the downside risk in the bad stocks. Does that sound like a good trade-off? It's your call. ❑

PLAY #83

Overwriting Long Positions

When a stock that I own has run up to the
overbought side of the bell curve, overwriting with
calls becomes a viable option strategy.

THIS IS A STRATEGY I often use. When I am long a particular stock and it has run up significantly in a short period of time, I often hedge the position. We discussed the bell curve and how a stock can statistically become overbought or oversold. When I find that a stock I own has run up to the overbought side of the bell curve, it suggests that its price probably will regress back to mean. This is a little tricky because regression to mean can happen in two ways: one, the stock falls back to the center of the bell curve, or two, it stays relatively neutral, and the calculation of the bell curve eventually mathematically shifts the stock back to center without the price changing much. I have experienced both cases.

Overwriting is simply selling a call option against a long position you might have in your portfolio. Basically, you have decided to rent your stock out, giving the buyer of the call you sold the right to take your stock anytime between the consummation of the trade and expiration date. If the stock falls back to the center of the bell curve during the life of the contract, you did a good thing. You have made your portfolio that much more productive by taking in the option premium. If the stock stays neutral during the life of the option, you also have done a good thing because the option expires worthless, allowing you to profit from the sale.

Here is where the strategy can go wrong, and it has often gone wrong with me when I have overwritten technology stocks. The stock cools off for a short period, and then gains its next injection of sponsorship (buying pressure), pushing it up to new highs—all during the life of the contract. Now you are faced with allowing the stock to be called away at expiration or buying back the option at a significant loss versus where you sold it. Of course, the underlying stock has made up the loss generated in the repurchase of the option, but that is on paper, and the loss on the call option is out of pocket. In many cases, one buys back the option at a loss, only to see the stock fall back to mean and force you to give up that paper profit that *was* offsetting the actual loss you took in the option.

I have a basic rule when I overwrite. I am perfectly prepared to give up the stock if it is called away so I don't get involved in buying back the option if it has gone against me. I simply allow the position to go to cash and then decide if I want to own the stock again. If so, I simply repurchase the stock. With commissions so low, I find this method works best for me. I always try to keep the options business simple. ❏

CHAPTER

OTHER INVESTMENT TIPS

THERE ARE NO PLAYOFFS, no Super Bowl or off-season, when it comes to your portfolio.

The market is an ever-present opponent that demands your continual preparation to play the investment game. The last eight chapters have provided you with a solid game plan, with numerous offensive and defensive plays.

From one season to the next, a football team's playbook is altered, with new plays being added and others subtracted. That new play might just be the "flea-flicker" or "Statue of Liberty." The following tips give you some new plays to add to your investment playbook.

The Job of the Fundamental Analyst

Increasing the odds of success means combining fundamental analysis with technical analysis, but to do that effectively, you must understand the job of the fundamental analyst.

FUNDAMENTALS ANSWER THE QUESTION of "what to buy," while technical analysis answers the question of "when to buy." It is important to understand the job of the fundamental analyst so that you can work as a team with the fundamentalist, each answering an important part of the equation. A recent article that I read had some important quotes and insight into the decision-making process of the fundamental analyst. Gretchen Morgenson, in her article, "How Did So Many Get It Wrong?" in the *New York Times* (December 31, 2000), does a great job pointing out exactly what is wrong with simply following fundamental research. She poses the question, "How can so many who are paid so much to scrutinize companies have blown it so spectacularly for their investor customers?"

The article goes on to suggest that one of the reasons for such poor research on Wall Street might be compression in commissions and fees. Brokerages have had to make up for this compression in other ways, such as investment banking business. This in itself has caused there to be only 29 sell recommendations out of 8,000 recommendations on the S&P 500 stocks, which is only half of 1 percent. The article was not very flattering of the fundamentalist's work, to say the least. In the article, Anthony Noto at Goldman, Sachs sums up the dilemma faced by fundamental analysts, and in doing so, points out why it is so important to incorporate technical analysis with your fundamental research.

Mr. Noto is an Internet analyst who rode the stocks he covers down into the low single digits in some cases. According to the arti-

cle, he is an analyst "who remained upbeat on shares that were trading at a fraction of their former values." The article goes on to say
he lowered his ratings on some stocks that had declined 98.2 percent during the previous fifty-two weeks. "Our research is driven by
fundamental analysis and is not influenced by anything else," Mr.
Noto said. He went on to explain that the companies he follows
saw their stock prices drop last spring not because their operations
were failing, but because market psychology had changed. He
downgraded the stocks much later because only then had it
become clear through his research that the companies' results
(fundamentals) were deteriorating. In hindsight, he said, "we
should have lowered our ratings sooner. We regret that."

Read that comment again, carefully, because Mr. Noto outlines
exactly what the problem is with using fundamental analysis by
itself. Fundamental analysis is a lagging indicator. In the quote
above, Mr. Noto, in essence, says that the stocks began to break
down technically before it became visible to him that the fundamentals were changing. It's like a baseball player waiting for a ball
to tag a runner out stealing a base. The third baseman is watching
the runner move closer by the second, but there is nothing he can
do to stop him until the outfielder throws the ball, and the ball
reaches his glove. Until that happens, he is helpless to stop the
runner from stealing third base.

For the fundamental analyst, the stocks he has recommended
may move lower each day, but he is helpless in stopping the car-
nage by lowering his rating on the stock until the fundamental
deterioration finally becomes evident. The company he follows is
not willing to give up that information until it is legally bound to do
so. Why give the analyst the information to downgrade your company until the last second? If the analyst had been able to use technical analysis along with his fundamental work he would have been
able to suggest hedging the stock at a minimum.

Noto said that market psychology had changed early on for
Internet stocks. Market psychology is technical analysis. When
market psychology turns bearish, more sell signals overtake buy
signals. Those who are watching can easily detect this subtle
change. Nothing is perfect, not even technical analysis, but trou-

ble will show up in the technical picture before it shows up in the fundamental picture, just as Mr. Noto says.

In view of this honest discussion by a top Wall Street analyst of how fundamental analysis is a lagging indicator, is there any question that you need to learn technical analysis? If you don't have any skills in the technical side, then you are doomed to wait until the fundamental deterioration shows up in stocks you own. Investors simply cannot afford to lose money this way again in the twenty-first century. What I find so interesting is that most firms keep these two schools of thought totally separate. The true key to success is using both schools of thought simultaneously. This, however, will not come to fruition on Wall Street as long as there are CFAs who view technical analysis as voodoo. ❑

PLAY #85

Being the Inventory Manager

Managing an investment portfolio is just like the inventory manager's job at the produce department or Macy's. The objective is to determine what season it is, and what will be the hot item that season.

OUR JOB AS STOCKBROKERS is a lot like that of an inventory manager. Think about it for a second. Nordstrom, Macy's, Target, and other such retailers own the store and the merchandise, and they are constantly rotating the inventory based on the season and consumer demand. A good inventory manager will bring out the merchandise before the season, not at the end. Once Halloween is over, then the Christmas promotional items will come out. A good inventory manager will know what the "hot" items for the gift-giving season will be—whether it is toys, electronic games, outdoor games, or clothes. Furthermore, a good inventory manager will make sure to have plenty of the popular items in stock. An item may be flying off the shelves, but if you don't have any inventory at your store, it's not going to help the bottom line.

In managing accounts, what we do is really all about inventory control. The first thing we must determine is what season it is. For this we turn to our sector rotation tools. When evaluating sectors, here are the indicators we look most heavily to:

Sector Bullish Percent
Sector Relative Strength
Percent of Stocks Whose RS Chart is in a Column of Xs (RSX)
Percent of Stocks Whose RS Chart is on a Buy Signal (RSP)
Percent of Stocks Whose Trends are Positive (PT)

Those sectors coming into season are indicated by a Sector Bullish Percent in Xs and by a good field position. Furthermore, the real leaders will be those sectors that have three or more of the Sector Relative Strength, RSX, RSP, and PT charts as positive and moving up.

The next step is deciding which items to place on the shelves. This is where individual stock selection comes into play. The catalog to order items from, so to speak, is our fundamental list of stocks. We use Value Line-ranked 1 and 2 stocks, as well as S&P-ranked 4 and 5 Stars as our catalog. There are many excellent fundamental research sites on the Internet that could be your "catalog."

Next comes your finesse as the inventory manager. This is where you determine which items will fly off the shelf that season. For this we look to find those stocks within the catalog inventory, the fundamental list, that have strong technical features. A simple method to start out with, which is highly effective, is to look for stocks whose relative strength chart is on a buy signal versus the market and its peers. These stocks should also have positive trends and be members of your fundamental list. Use the chart pattern and the relative strength chart to manage the inventory. When an item stops selling in the store, you pull it off the shelves and replace it with something that is selling. The same is true in your portfolio. As you constantly re-evaluate the portfolio, you are pulling out stocks with deteriorating relative strength or with negative trend changes, while replacing it with stocks whose trend charts are healthy and have good relative strength. ❏

When Old Meets New: An Alternative to the Dogs of the Dow

An old dog can be taught new tricks.

ON NOVEMBER 1, 1999, Dow Jones changed four stocks in its benchmark index, the Dow Jones Industrial Average (DJIA). The four components of the index are now Microsoft (MSFT), Intel (INTC), SBC Communications (SBC), and Home Depot (HD). One could easily argue that these changes are a little late; the addition of more technology names should have been made sooner to reflect the growing importance of technology in our economy. In fact, it would not surprise us if the Nasdaq Composite continued on its upward movement and surpassed the price of the DJIA in the next ten years. That's not out of the question. The average annual gain of the DJIA for the last five years is 25.71 percent, and the average gain of the Nasdaq Composite is 41.89 percent. If you extrapolate that out, at the end of the year in 2008, the Nasdaq Composite would be higher priced than the DJIA. Nonetheless, the recent changes in the Dow Jones should have you wondering if the "Dogs of the Dow" is necessarily the right strategy to use in the coming years.

The basic premise of the Dogs of the Dow is sound. The theory is to buy down-and-out stocks and then to hold one year, keeping "the fingers out of the pie," so to speak, giving the strategy a chance to work. As the DJIA is changing, dividend yield, normally used in choosing the Dogs of the Dow, is not such a good measure anymore. Companies are rewarding investors with higher stock prices via stock buybacks and stock options, as well as putting money back into operations, versus paying dividends. The tax laws also make it more advantageous for the investor to be rewarded with a higher stock price than dividends. Therefore, new ways of evaluating the stocks that go into a five-stock Dow portfolio should be investigated.

One of the things that all technicians can agree upon is that relative strength is an important tool, no matter how you measure it. In the point and figure method, the stock's relative strength chart is depicted with buy and sell signals and columns of Xs and Os. In the Dow Relative Strength theory, instead of the first cut being determined by dividends, we decided to take a look at relative strength. This does one thing that becomes even more important today—it allows every stock the opportunity to be a part of the portfolio.

At this writing, there are eleven stocks that yield less than 1 percent, and they are some of the big winners over time, like Wal-Mart, Microsoft, Home Depot, Intel, etc. This makes it close to impossible to ever see them in the Dividend Dogs of the Dow strategy. The next step in the strategy is to pick the five lowest-priced stocks. This attempts to buy down-and-out stocks that are coming back around. Finally, we hold the portfolio for one year. We call this the Relative Strength 5 Theory.

The Relative Strength 5 Theory uses the tenets of the Dogs of the Dow that work, but updates the strategy to reflect the changing economy and the changing markets. If you never changed the DJIA from its inception in 1896 as thirty stocks, then you would have a lot of out-of-business companies. Here are the basic principles in the construction of the Relative Strength 5 Theory.

SETTING UP THE PORTFOLIO

THE STRATEGY IS pretty simple. First, start with Dow Jones stocks. Second, narrow the list down to those stocks whose relative strength charts are in a column of Xs. Third, rank the stocks by price to find the five lowest priced. Fourth, buy equal dollar amounts in each stock and hold for one year.

FAMILIARITY

EVERYONE KNOWS THE companies in the DJIA. These are large-cap stocks with well-known brand names.

RELATIVE STRENGTH

THE RELATIVE STRENGTH concept is something we have found to be very important in stock selection. The relative strength chart shows us which stocks are performing better relative to the overall market. In the Relative Strength 5 Strategy, the first criterion is that the stock must be in a column of Xs on its relative strength chart. This tells us the stock is outperforming the market.

PRICE

BUYING THE FIVE lowest-priced stocks of those in a column of Xs attempts to get those stocks into the portfolio that have been down and out, but are turning around.

ONE YEAR

ONCE YOU HAVE determined the stocks for the Relative Strength 5 Theory, you buy equal dollar amounts and then hold for one year. Holding for one year keeps the "fingers out of the pie" and gives the stocks enough time to work out.

ALL STOCKS ARE CANDIDATES

ONE HUGE ADVANTAGE of the Relative Strength 5 Theory over the Dogs of the Dow is that every stock has an opportunity to be in the portfolio. With the Dogs of the Dow, the stock must pay a dividend to qualify. Some of the great performers like Coca-Cola, McDonald's, Wal-Mart, and now Intel, Microsoft, and Home Depot don't ever get a chance to be in the Dogs of the Dow because they don't pay a high-enough dividend compared to the others. Now that fewer than one-third of the stocks in the DJIA yield more than 1 percent, there isn't a lot of turnover year to year in the Dogs of the Dow portfolio. You don't have that problem with the Relative Strength 5 portfolio.

ADJUNCT TO THE DOW 10

IF YOU USUALLY HAVE done the Dow 10 Strategy, you might want to consider doing the Dogs of the Dow 5 with the Relative Strength 5. You still end up with a group of ten stocks from the Dow Jones, but you not only get some dividend stocks, but also stocks that are showing good performance relative to the overall market. Typically the stocks in the Dogs of the Dow and the Relative Strength 5 are different, so you don't have to worry about overlap between the two portfolios.

PERFORMANCE

THE RESULTS OF our internal back testing on the strategy have shown that the Relative Strength 5 Strategy performs quite well. We began testing on December 31, 1987, because that is how far back we have data. Had you invested $10,000 on December 31, 1987, in each strategy, the figures below are what your portfolio would be worth as of December 31, 1999. Again, the results include dividends but no commissions.

These results were calculated by taking the five lowest-priced Dow Jones stocks that were in a column of Xs on their RS charts as of December 31st of each year and buying equal dollar amounts and holding for one year. We then assumed that the stocks were sold at the end of each year and the proceeds were rolled into the new picks. Dividends are included in the calcula-

Dow Relative Strength Study Results

YEAR	DJIA	RS 5	DOGS OF DOW
1988	16.00%	21.41%	18.40%
1989	31.70	23.39	10.50
1990	-0.40	-6.71	-15.20
1991	23.90	44.47	61.79
1992	7.40	18.72	22.88
1993	16.80	20.26	33.82
1994	4.90	-2.53	8.08
1995	36.40	46.61	30.26
1996	28.20	18.09	26.00
1997	22.64	21.83	18.98
1998	16.10	26.97	12.32
1999	25.22	32.89	-4.83

As of 12/31/99, results if you had invested $10,000 on December 31, 1987:

$77,334	$99,997	$66,592

tions but no commissions or sales charges are deducted. These results have not been audited, and, of course, past performance is not indicative of future performance. ❑

PLAY #87

Investing in Dividend
Re-Investment Plans (DRIPs)

DRIPs are a great way to get your feet wet with investing.

WHAT IS A DRIP? It is a dividend re-investment plan. You hear stories suggesting that if you had just saved $10 a month and invested it in a company like McDonald's how rich you would be, or if you had bought one share of Microsoft and held on how it would be worth a zillion dollars. It makes a great story and sounds like a great idea, but how can you invest $10 in a $70 stock? DRIPs are how you do it.

This is the neat thing about these plans. They do not require a large sum of money to get started. These programs differ from company to company, but you can often start by buying as little as $100 worth of stock directly from the company. The company then reinvests the dividends for the individual by buying additional shares, or a fraction of shares in most cases, without a fee. These days there is typically a fee associated with the sale of the shares, but it is often minimal.

This is a great way for the small individual investor to start to build a portfolio of blue-chip stocks, and there are many to choose from. There are more than 1,200 companies that have DRIP programs.

Since this is primarily a strategy of buy and hold, be sure to do your fundamental homework to make sure it is a company that will be around for the long haul. From a technical standpoint, consider looking at companies that have positive relative strength (RS) and that are trading above their bullish support lines. The RS will help identify stocks that are outperforming the averages, and the stocks that are trading above their bullish support lines have a positive trend.

This may also be a great tool to help you educate your kids as well as save for their college tuition. There are a lot of companies kids are familiar with (sometimes too familiar), but they can really relate to these companies and get excited about being an owner. I think it's a great opportunity to use that excitement and curiosity to teach them more about the companies they have an interest in, as well as some of the basics of investing. With so many DRIPs to choose from and the low cost involved, you can almost certainly find a company or two that captures your youngsters' interest.

If there is a company you are interested in, visit its Web site. There you will find information about its DRIP, along with details about minimums and fees. ❏

PLAY # 88

Cocktail Party Indicator

Don't forget to have a good time, too.

THE STOCK MARKET IS an interesting being. We say *being* because it seems to have a life of its own, though it acts contrary to what many investors think. For example, if Wal-Mart were to have a huge sale offering 25 percent off every item in the store, the lines waiting to get into the stores would be unbelievable. On the other hand, if the stock market has a 25-percent-off sale, no one is around. Everyone is scared to death. That is why we say the market acts contrary.

You may find the same thing as you attend parties or cookouts. The stock market can be the talk of the party, as it was in 1999 with Internet stocks, or it may not even come up, except in less than glowing terms. It may be possible that you can use these parties to extract a small dose of investment advice with a "Cocktail Party Bullish Percent Index." This is derived using the NYSE Bullish Percent and where it stands at a given period of time. You may want to keep a copy of this handy, just in case you need it for reference purposes. ❏

Cocktail Party Bullish Percent Index

EVENT

Your best friend and neighbor has a cocktail party to which you are not invited.

A friend invites you to a cocktail party. However, when the other guests see you, they move to the other side of the room.

You are attending a cocktail party. People who know you come over to ask how the market closed today and what you think they should buy.

You are attending a cocktail party. When people hear you are an investment adviser they come over and introduce themselves and discuss the market.

A client invites you to a cocktail party. When you enter the room he asks everyone to be quiet for a moment while he introduces you to all assembled as "his investment adviser."

Your best friend invites you to a cocktail party and dinner in your honor.

MARKET DIRECTION

The market is at the bottom. Call all of your clients and tell them to buy, if anyone will answer the phone. Market just had a 6 percent reversal to the upside from below the 30 percent level.

The market is in a basing formation and will rally shortly. Market just reversed up to Bull Alert status and is ready to rally.

The market is in a major upswing. Just moved into Bull Confirmed status and crossed the 50 percent level.

The market has had a large rally and is now receiving good group rotation. The Bullish Percent is rising and nearing the 70 percent level. Offensive team doing well.

The market is nearing a top. A reversal from a lower high with the Bullish Percent Index around the overbought 70 percent level.

The market has reached the top. Call your clients the next morning and tell them to sell everything. Of course, they won't, as they will think you are kidding. Therefore, sell everything you own so you will have the money to buy your own drinks as the market drops back below the 30 percent level on the Bullish Percent Index.

PLAY # 8 9

All I Needed to Know I Learned from Noah's Ark

One of our clients e-mailed us a list of homilies entitled
"All I Needed to Know I Learned from Noah's Ark."
Here's our take on how these life lessons tie in
with a disciplined approach to investing.

◆ **Plan ahead.** It wasn't raining when Noah built the ark. It is important to remember that the NYSE Bullish Percent and other indicators are leading indicators. They look forward with respect to the market. The Bullish Percent takes in all of the things happening in the world, things we may not understand just yet, and compiles them together. The indicators are designed to be bearish at the top and bullish at the bottom. They are designed to have turned the corner earlier so you have time to prepare, whereas the financial news media reports on what has happened or is happening right now.

◆ **Stay fit.** The best way to "stay fit" with the point and figure methodology is to chart your top twenty holdings by hand everyday. This forces you to become a craftsman in this methodology. There is no better way to get to know a stock than to chart it every day. No sell signals and no buy signals will escape you. We still chart some stocks by hand everyday at DWA, even though the computer system does 8,000 stocks. We look at ourselves as craftsmen supported by computers.

◆ **Don't listen to critics—do what has to be done.** Stick to your game plan. No system is going to work perfectly 100 percent of the time. But you must find a system that you believe in and stick with it. Back in the spring of 2000, there were lots of people espousing the merits of buying "momentum stocks." You know—the buy-high-and-hope-to-sell-higher school of thought. Well, that bubble was burst, all right. By going back to the old adage, buy low and sell high, you are sticking to the solid principles of economics. You might be using the hottest, newest craze in town, but through thick and thin, buying low and selling high has never hurt anyone.

◆ **Build on high ground.** The best thing you can do for yourself in business is to be a businessperson with the highest morals and integrity. Always take the high road, and you'll be better off for it in the end.

◆ **For safety's sake, travel in pairs.** You achieve the best results when you put the fundamentals and the technicals together. Fundamentals tell you what to buy, and the technicals tell you when. The goal is to stack as many odds in your favor as possible. There are countless examples of stocks that continued to plunge despite having solid company fundamentals. It comes back to the law of supply and demand, which can easily be seen in the point and figure chart. The best successes come when both the fundamentals and technicals are in sync.

◆ **Speed isn't always an advantage.** The cheetahs were on board, but so were the snails. It can seem enticing to play the Junipers (JNPR) and Aribas (ARBA) or whatever the "hot" stock of the moment is, but don't forget that as fast as they rally, they can fall twice as fast. In 2000, the electric utility sector reversed up from the "green zone" to give a buy signal early in 2000, and the sector posted a 40 percent return for the year. Of course, electric utilities are not "sexy" to talk about at cocktail parties. As we always say, you move ahead twenty yards, and then the market takes back fifteen. There is a reason that the average return over the last sixty years is about 12 percent.

◆ **If you can't fight or flee—float!** Most investors have had a stock go against them at some point. That doesn't mean you just give up on the game and sink. Instead, you address the situation head-on. One answer might be to sell calls against the stock to take the sell decision away from you. Maybe the stock is at its support line and due for a bounce; use the bounce to come out. Maybe you stick a stop-loss point in so you can get out when you can't take the heat any longer. Maybe you swap the symbol—sell that stock and go into another at the same price, which has a much better probability of moving higher. There are lots of things you can do to be proactive rather than reactive.

◆ **Take care of your animals as if they were the last ones on earth.** Treat your stocks with respect. If you own a stock that breaks a triple bottom, violates the bullish support line and the relative strength turns negative, heed the advice. That stock has done everything it can to tell us something is wrong. The reverse is also true. When you have a sector that reverses up on its bullish percent chart and the relative strength is improving, plus you see a number of stocks with good patterns that are positive, it is telling you something about what's going on in that group. Listen.

◆ **Don't forget that we're all in the same boat.** One of the philosophies of our firm is "You can't keep it unless you give it away." Education is very important. It has been our mission since this company was started in 1987 to educate stockbrokers and to provide them with a sensible, logical, and organized game plan with which to invest in the market. Brokers, educate your clients. Individual investors, educate your friends and your family. When you help others to be the best they can be, it will always come back to you tenfold.

◆ **When the garbage gets really deep, don't sit there and complain—shovel!** This is one of my favorites. When the market is tough, as it was in 2000, it is hard to face the prospects of managing your account. However, addressing the portfolio today means tomorrow is much easier. Often, once you decide to take action on the first troubling position, you'll find it easier to address other problem situations. Don't just let a position that is not working atrophy. Address it immediately.

◆ **Stay below deck during the storm.** When the storm is brewing, take action. Don't sit on your laurels and expect someone else to take care of you. When the NYSE or OTC Bullish Percent goes to defense, that's your call to attention. It's time for action. You might decide to sell calls, just forgo any further buying, initiate stop loss points, take partial positions off the table, etc. The point is that you boarded up the windows and bought some canned goods and extra bottled water. It doesn't mean that you won't have some wind or rain damage, but you did everything you could to mitigate that risk.

◆ **Remember that the ark was built by amateurs and the Titanic was built by professionals.** The wonderful thing about the stock market is it keeps us humble. When you start to get too confident that you have this whole thing figured out, the market has a way of coming in and knocking you down a notch. We stick to that KISS principle: Keep it simple, silly. We don't try to get too complicated. We keep our list of indicators short. We stick to the same principles that govern the produce in the supermarket—supply and demand.

◆ **If you have to start over, have a friend by your side.** You must adopt a methodology that you believe in. It could be Fibonacci numbers, Gann angles, astrology, or point and figure. We subscribe to the point and figure methodology because it is rooted in the irrefutable law of supply and demand. Whatever methodology you choose, you must have a game plan and stick to it. Nothing ever works 100 percent of the time. If you constantly keep hunting for the perfect methodology, it will not get you where you want to go. Success requires staying focused and disciplined.

◆ **Remember that the woodpeckers *inside* are often a bigger threat than the storm *outside*.** When the Bullish Percents make a major change, it is always a gut-wrenching experience. You go home with a knot in your stomach as you think of all of the reasons it is going to fail you this time. You must stay focused, though. This is the whole reason for having indicators. Otherwise, you're just going on gut instinct and emotion.

◆ **Don't miss the boat.** To survive in the investment business you will need to become a craftsman. Find something and become an expert in it. Learning this methodology well will take you through your investing career. It does take some time and effort. You don't just plug the program into the computer, hit a key, and see the magical answer appear before you. This is an art, not a science. But if you think about anything in your life that is worthwhile, you've had to work for it. This is no different.

◆ **No matter how bleak it looks, there's always a rainbow on the other side.** When the NYSE Bullish Percent, OTC Bullish Percent, or any of the sector bullish percents is down and out, having fallen from above 70 percent down to the oversold territory, and just about all of the stocks out there are beaten up, therein lies opportunity. Of course, on the nightly business news they are going to be talking about recession and depression, but when the Bullish Percent reverses up from below 30 percent, it presents an opportunity that doesn't come along every day, and it suggests the odds are on your side for upside potential. ❑

To Be Successful, Continually Educate Yourself

The theory of supply and demand is an unwavering economic principle. Although this theory is static in concept, we continually evolve and adapt to the ever-changing market conditions and therefore are constantly developing new ways to depict the battle between supply and demand.

ABOUT THE ONLY THING that does not change in this world is the law of supply and demand, which is at the heart of the point and figure methodology. Yet, how the charts are interpreted and the tools we use to evaluate the supply and demand relationship are constantly changing. Patterns do not change, but the importance placed on them, as well as some of the indicators, are constantly being worked and reworked. This is where the point and figure methodology becomes an art form rather than a science. To be a good craftsman, you must constantly educate yourself on the subtle changes and the new tools available.

The concept behind bullish percent charts does not change, but the sectors we keep bullish percent charts on change as the market dictates. Recently, new sectors like the Internet have been introduced. We have developed new indicator charts like the percent of stocks with positive trend or weekly distribution charts to meet changing needs. These new tools are not changes in the methodology, but rather new ways to depict the battle between supply and demand.

Do not assume there's nothing new to learn. The point and figure methodology may have been around for a hundred years, but it is still being recreated every day. ❑

GLOSSARY

Bear Alert. Characterized by a bullish percent falling from above 70 percent to below. Profits should be taken or positions hedged. The traffic light has turned red.

Bear Confirmed. The weakest of market conditions. Characterized by a column of Os exceeding a previous column of Os. The traffic light is red.

Bear Correction. The bear market is taking a breather. Trading rallies could be seen but the bear market will likely resume. The traffic light is flashing red—look both ways carefully before crossing the intersection.

Bearish Catapult. A triple bottom breakdown followed by a double bottom breakdown.

Bearish Signal Reversed. A stock makes a series of lower highs and lower lows but abruptly, without a period of accumulation, "reverses" this "bearish" pattern and breaks out. This pattern carries a very high probability the stock will move higher, quickly.

Bearish Triangle. A stock makes a series of lower highs and higher lows to actually form what looks like a triangle. The stock comes to a point at which it must break to the upside or downside. Usually a stock in a downtrend will breakout to the downside and complete the bearish triangle. A breakout from a triangle pattern usually results in a quick, explosive move. The pattern must be at least five columns wide.

Bull Alert. Characterized by the bullish percent falling to 30 percent or below and then reversing up into a column of Xs. The traffic light turns green.

Bull Confirmed. The strongest of market conditions. Characterized by a column of Xs exceeding a previous column of Xs. The traffic light is green.

Bull Correction. The bull market is taking a breather, though it should resume shortly. The traffic light is yellow.

Bullish Catapult. A triple top breakout followed by a double top breakout.

Bullish Signal Reversed. A stock makes a series of higher highs and higher lows but abruptly, without a period of accumulation, "reverses" this "bullish" pattern and breaks down. This pattern carries a very high probability the stock will move lower.

Bullish Triangle. A stock makes a series of lower highs and higher lows to actually form what looks like a triangle. The stock comes to a point at which it must break to the upside or downside. Usually a stock in an uptrend will breakout to the upside and complete the bullish triangle. A breakout from a triangle pattern usually results in a quick, explosive move. The pattern must be at least five columns wide.

Double Bottom. The most basic of all sell signals. Characterized by a column of Os exceeding a previous column of Os.

Double Top. The most basic of all buy signals. Characterized by a column of Xs exceeding a previous column of Xs.

High Pole Warning. A column of Xs exceeds a previous column of Xs by at least three boxes and then retraces the previous up move by more than 50 percent. Used in evaluating the Dow Jones 20 Bond Average. The High Pole Warning is considered a sell signal.

Industry Groups Bullish Percent. This is the same concept as the NYSE Bullish Percent. The percent of stocks on buy signals in each sector is plotted on a grid from 0 percent to 100 percent. The best buy signals come when a sector goes below 30 percent and then reverses up. The best sell signals come when a sector goes above 70 percent and then reverses below 70 percent. The same six risk levels apply.

Low Pole Warning. A stock or index exceeds a previous column of

Os by at least three boxes and then retraces the previous down-move by more than 50 percent. This buy signal is often used when evaluating Advance-Decline charts, or the Dow Jones 20 Bond Average chart.

Momentum Change. The price the stock needs to hit in order to change its momentum. If the price of the stock is below this change number then the change number is where the momentum will turn positive. If the price of the stock is above the change number then this is where the weekly momentum will turn negative.

NYSE Bullish Percent. The best buy signals come when the NYSE Bullish Percent goes below 30 percent and then reverses up. The best sell signals come when the indicator moves above 70 percent and then reverses below 70 percent. There are six degrees of risk associated with this indicator: Bull Alert, Bull Confirmed, Bull Correction, Bear Alert, Bear Confirmed, and Bear Correction.

NYSE High-Low Index. The number of new highs made on the NYSE divided by the number of new highs plus new lows. This number is then recorded on a ten-day moving average. The ten-day moving average is then plotted on a grid from 0 percent to 100 percent. The best buy signals come when this indicator falls below 30 percent and reverses up. The best sell signals come when the indicator reverses from above to below 70 percent.

Percent of Stocks above Their 10-Week Moving Average. One of our two main short-term indicators. The best buy signals come when this indicator goes below 30 percent and then reverses up. The best sell signals comes when this indicator goes above 70 percent and then reverses to below 70 percent.

Relative Strength. The relative strength reading is calculated by taking the price of the stock and dividing by the DJIA and then multiplying by 1,000. This number is then plotted on a point and figure chart. Buy signals are given when a column of Xs exceeds a previous column of Xs. Sell signals are given when a column of Os exceeds a previous column of Os. Relative strength signals generally last about two years and tell the overall trend of a stock. Positive relative strength suggests the stock will outperform the market while negative relative strength suggests the stock will underperform the market. Its also important to watch for reversals for short term guidance.

Trading Band. The basic bell curve. 100 percent overbought or "Top" is three standard deviations above normal. 100 percent oversold is three standard deviations below normal. If the stock is 100 percent overbought, it suggests the stock will correct to normal on the curve. If the stock is 100 percent oversold, it suggests the stock will bounce to normal. The disadvantage to trading bands is the tails can go out to infinity.

Triple Bottom. A stock forms support at a level twice. On the third test of this support, the stock is unable to hold and violates that support level. Generally this is a negative formation.

Triple Top. A stock forms resistance at a level twice. On the third test of this resistance, the stock is able to penetrate resistance by at least one box. Generally this is a positive formation.

Weekly Momentum. This is a one-week versus five-week moving average that is exponentially weighted and then smoothed. The exact calculation is proprietary information. The weekly momentum is very helpful when timing trades. A positive weekly momentum suggests higher prices and negative momentum suggests lower prices. Weekly momentum is a shorter term timing tool, as changes to positive or negative weekly momentum last seven weeks on average.

About the Authors

THOMAS J. DORSEY

ORIGINALLY FROM BOSTON, Thomas Dorsey traveled the globe at a young age, being the son of a career Army man. After serving in the Navy during the Vietnam War, Dorsey graduated from Virginia Commonwealth University with a degree in Business Administration and Economics. It was the economics theory of supply and demand that drew him to the point and figure methodology. Prior to founding Dorsey, Wright & Associates, Dorsey worked at Merrill Lynch and Wheat, First Securities.

Dorsey, along with Wright, were recognized as co-finalists for The 1999 Richmond Chamber of Commerce Small Business Man of the Year award, as well as co-finalists for the 1999 Virginia Ernst & Young Entrepreneur(s) of the Year award.

With Dorsey, Wright's focus on the education of their clientele, Dorsey has spoken across the world on risk management and specifically the point and figure methodology. He was bestowed the Distinguished Speaker Award from the Wharton School of Finance Industry Associates.

He is the author of two prior works, *Point and Figure Charting: The Essential Application for Forecasting and Tracking Market Prices* (Wiley, 1995), and *Thriving as a Stockbroker in the 21st Century* (Bloomberg Press, 1999). In addition, he has been interviewed by or has authored articles for *The Wall Street Journal, Barron's, Fortune, Bloomberg Personal, Futures,* and *Technical Analysis of Stocks and Commodities.*

Dorsey's other interests include riding his custom Harley Davidson, being a hot-air balloon pilot, and, especially, weight lifting. He has won state titles in his age group for the Bench Press, Dead Lift, and Squat. In addition, he is the American AAU and World AAU record holder for Power Lifting (50–55 years).

Dorsey and his wife, Cindy, have three children, Thomas, Mitchell, and Samantha.

WATSON H. WRIGHT

WATSON WRIGHT WAS RAISED in Petersburg, Virginia. He graduated from Washington and Lee University in 1977 with a B.S. in

Business Administration. He began his career in the brokerage industry in the fall of that year, starting as a stockbroker at Wheat, First Securities in the Petersburg, Virginia, office. In March 1978, Wright had an opportunity to work briefly for the head of the firm's research department. It was during this time that he first encountered and began to learn point and figure charting. One of his daily duties was charting every stock that the research department followed.

Wright remained a stockbroker until the summer of 1981. At that time, he left the brokerage side to begin working for Tom Dorsey in the Options Strategy Department. He remained in that capacity through 1986, when he left Wheat, First Securities to help co-found Dorsey, Wright & Associates.

Along with Tom Dorsey, Wright was a co-finalist in the 1999 Virginia Ernest & Young Entrepreneur of the Year awards, and they were also finalists in the 1999 Richmond Chamber of Commerce Small Businessman of the Year award.

Wright and his wife, Allison, have three children, Forrest, Watson, Jr., and Meredith.

SUSAN L. MORRISON

SUSAN L. MORRISON, vice president, has been an analyst with Dorsey, Wright & Associates (DWA) for thirteen years. She joined the firm as the first associate in September 1987, only months after the firm was started. Prior to that, Morrison worked in the Municipal Bond Department at Signet Bank and Signet's Trust Company. In the early years, Morrison not only worked for DWA full time, but concurrently attended Virginia Commonwealth University (VCU) majoring in Finance and Economics. She graduated in 1989.

Over the years, Morrison has become a true craftsman in technical analysis, and in particular has become an expert in the point and figure methodology. She provides daily written market commentary to the firm's flagship product, "The Daily Equity & Market Analysis Report." In addition, she runs the "Trader's Corner," which is a monitored short-term trading program for DWA's professional clients. Morrison is considered the stock picker for the firm, and is the one everyone relies on for a consistent flow of stock ideas and recommendations.

Besides writing research commentary for other DWA products, Morrison serves as the liaison between DWA Research and the DWA Money Management subsidiary. She also comanages the firm's profit sharing account, commodity trading account, and other money management trading accounts.

Morrison also teaches point and figure charting seminars across the country and internationally, in particular for DWA's Broker Institute. In addition, she conducts in-house research projects on the subject of point and figure charting in an effort to keep Dorsey, Wright on the cutting edge of technical analysis.

JAMES C. BALL

BORN AND RAISED IN VIRGINIA, James Ball, vice president, attended the Virginia Military Institute (VMI), graduating in 1986 with a B.S. in Civil Engineering. While in school, his involvement with the Cadet Investment Group solidified his desire to be in the investment business. Deciding not to pursue a career in his field of education, he went to New York shortly after completing VMI to work on a taxable fixed-income trading desk at a large brokerage house.

Four years later, Ball and his family decided to move back to Virginia. Thomas Dorsey hired him in 1990 as an analyst. His responsibilities include writing commentary for the daily equity reports, as well as developing new tools to enhance DWA research.

In addition to analyst duties, he has overseen the growth and development of Dorsey Wright's internal information systems. The system has grown from three stand-alone PCs to a multiserver network. Ball has also managed the development of www.dorseywright.com, which has become one of the world's largest Internet point and figure charting resources.

Ball and his wife, Jennifer, have three sons, Jamie, Alec, and Taylor.

TAMMY F. DEROSIER

TAMMY DEROSIER, vice president, became a Dorsey, Wright analyst in 1992, yet her association with the company began in 1988. DeRosier started as a part-time employee, gaining valuable experience throughout her college tenure before coming aboard full-time after graduation. She graduated from The McIntire School of Commerce at the University of Virginia with a B.S. in Finance and Marketing and a minor in Sociology.

DeRosier is a daily contributor to the firm's principal research report, "The Daily Equity and Market Analysis Report." She also regularly authors other proprietary reports and research columns on the firm's Web site. DeRosier comanages the firm's profit sharing account and conducts in-house research, such as developing the Dorsey, Wright Relative Strength 5 theory.

Developing, organizing, and conducting several different types of seminar formats is a main responsibility for DeRosier. These courses are based on her discussions about point and figure methodology with investment professionals and individual investors across the world. DeRosier has also been featured on local television shows as well as in newspaper and Web articles.

DeRosier and her husband, Scott, reside just outside Richmond, Virginia, where she was born and raised.

About Bloomberg

Bloomberg L.P., founded in 1981, is a global information services, news, and media company. Headquartered in New York, the company has nine sales offices, two data centers, and 79 news bureaus worldwide.

Bloomberg, serving customers in 100 countries around the world, holds a unique position within the financial services industry by providing an unparalleled range of features in a single package known as the BLOOMBERG PROFESSIONAL™ service. By addressing the demand for investment performance and efficiency through an exceptional combination of information, analytic, electronic trading, and Straight Through Processing tools, Bloomberg has built a worldwide customer base of corporations, issuers, financial intermediaries, and institutional investors.

BLOOMBERG NEWS℠, founded in 1990, provides stories and columns on business, general news, politics, and sports to leading newspapers and magazines throughout the world. BLOOMBERG TELEVISION®, a 24-hour business and financial news network, is produced and distributed globally in seven different languages. BLOOMBERG RADIO™ is an international radio network anchored by flagship station BLOOMBERG® WBBR 1130 in New York.

In addition to the BLOOMBERG PRESS® line of books, Bloomberg publishes *BLOOMBERG® MARKETS, BLOOMBERG PERSONAL FINANCE™,* and *BLOOMBERG® WEALTH MANAGER.* To learn more about Bloomberg, call a sales representative at:

Frankfurt:	49-69-92041-200	São Paulo:	5511-3048-4530
Hong Kong:	85-2-2977-6600	Singapore:	65-212-1200
London:	44-20-7330-7500	Sydney:	61-2-9777-8601
New York:	1-212-318-2200	Tokyo:	81-3-3201-8950
San Francisco:	1-415-912-2980		

FOR IN-DEPTH MARKET INFORMATION and news, visit BLOOMBERG.COM®, which draws from the news and power of the BLOOMBERG PROFESSIONAL™ service and Bloomberg's host of media products to provide high-quality news and information in multiple languages on stocks, bonds, currencies, and commodities, at **www.bloomberg.com.**